The Crucifixion of Jesus
Was it Really Friday?
Does it Really Matter?

Buck Hurlbut

DEDICATION

This is dedicated to my wife Mary, son Landon and daughter Abby, without whom my life would be very empty; to the memory of my mother Frances who was the first in our family to know Jesus as Lord and who encouraged me to do the same; to the Holy Spirit whose patience, counselling and teaching through my walk with Jesus has been my lifeline; and to Jesus through whom our family line has been forever changed.

Table of Contents

The Post-sacrificial Events _____ 63

Three Day Learning   83

ix

ACKNOWLEDGMENTS

I extend special thanks to Blue Letter Bible for their spectacular app, website and research tools. I cannot fully express my gratitude for the labor you've invested to make God's word and resources so accessible for those of us who love to study. Thank you.

WHY DOES FRIDAY MATTER?

It's never made sense to me how Jesus could die on a Friday afternoon and be resurrected before sunrise on Sunday, because those events don't allow Jesus to fulfill His prophetic self-identification with Jonah (i.e. "For as Jonas was three days and three nights in the whale's belly; so shall the Son of man be three days and three nights in the heart of the earth." – Mt 12:40). Does this prophecy matter? It seems strange that Jesus would say it and then humanity would marginalize it. We don't treat Jesus' other words as optional, so why these? Some have tried to work around this Friday to Sunday inconsistency by saying the Jewish calendar tracks days differently, which is indeed true; however, three days are three days and three nights are three nights irrespective of how you track them: three of each is three of each, and a Friday afternoon crucifixion with a Sunday morning resurrection won't work.

I also wondered about the events of the Passover celebration and some seeming inconsistencies as I watched this defining celebration unfold with Jesus in the midst. The Passover is a huge part of the crucifixion account. Jesus celebrated the Passover, as did all the main Jewish players in the crucifixion timeline (priests, Jewish leaders, disciples): they were all very staunch supporters of the feast because improper keeping of the feast was grounds for expulsion from the nation of Israel. God didn't leave much in the way of room for a Jew to improperly celebrate the Passover. Because of this, celebrating the Passover was a keystone to the Jewish culture then, and still is to this day. Even the Roman government at the time was respectful of the Jewish celebration of Passover, because doing so relieved tremendous political tension.

I've been a systems analyst for 30 years, a follower of Jesus and a student of the Scripture for 40, and after not being able to reconcile these differences, I decided to analyze every Scripture I could on the resurrection and Passover events to see what they said and to adjust my understanding with more in-depth learning of both. I set my pre-conceived understandings and past church learning aside. To more fully grasp what happened, I decided to place all the Passover and resurrection related gospel Scripture in sequence, starting from the oldest events, working up to the resurrection itself and then advancing beyond, keeping an eye for patterns and oddities. I let my curiosity drive my study. My hope was that by putting the events in sequence, I could observe, from Scripture only, what really happened and when. I was not disappointed. My core understanding has been forever changed and I will never see the account of Jesus' crucifixion, the Passover or the resurrection events the same way again, and I'm glad.

All Calendars Are Not Alike

The most formidable challenge I faced, and still do when reading and discussing the Passover and resurrection events, is the difference between my culture's and the Jewish religious culture's way of tracking the beginning and ending of a day. Much of the world uses the Gregorian calendar that was introduced in 1582 and which was created from the Roman calendar before it. The Gregorian calendar has continued to grow as a globally accepted calendar system ever since. You may not have known that the system used to create the calendar hanging on your refrigerator, with its method for tracking days and months, even had a name, but if you use a calendar that follows the "30 days has September, April, June and November" rhetoric, you're using a Gregorian calendar. It is based on 24 equal, 60-minute hours from midnight to midnight, comprising 12 months, with a total of 365 and ¼ days per year on average.

This system of tracking, however, is not the only way to track days and many eastern people groups track days differently; this is certainly true of the Jewish culture as it applies to its religious practices. According to the book of Genesis, biblical days begin in the evening, progress through morning and end at the beginning of the next evening. This is the day format prescribed by God, that is followed by Judaism's religious observances now, and which was the only calendar they followed during Jesus' lifetime. Remember, our current Gregorian calendar did not emerge until 1582.

To Jesus, the day began at sunset, making supper the first meal of a new day. Evening is considered sundown to sunup and morning is considered sunup to sundown; so, 3PM is still considered the morning period of the day. I found that I was battling my own perceptions of days and times and that those deep perceptions were so instinctual that they were hindering me from understanding the chronology of the Scripture. An example of this difference between the Gregorian calendar and the calendar of the gospels is illustrated in Jn 12 when Jesus travels to see Mary, Martha and Lazarus and they make supper for Him. In my 24-hour, midnight-to-midnight mind, it's all the same day, but on the Jewish calendar used during Jesus' life, and that is still used for religious practices today, it's two days: the day He came and the next day when He sat to eat supper. The transition from one day to the next illustratively happened between the time that Jesus stood up to wash His hands for supper and the time He sat down to eat it, just as the sun set.

You may believe that changing your day and time mindset is as simple as flipping a switch, but it's not. You have to *practice* a new way of thinking for it to become normal. Even after months of study, I still find myself relying on my deeply engrained western mindset and find myself triple checking my understanding of the Scripture as I read. The issue comes from trying to force the Jewish evening-to-evening narrative into a midnight-to-midnight Gregorian calendar. When we remove the Gregorian calendar from the process of interpreting the Scripture account, the gospel narrative falls into place. Instead of using Monday, Tuesday and Wednesday to identify when something happened, we evaluate the Scriptures in their own light with events relative to each other and based on the sunset to sunset day structure that was observed when the Scripture accounts happened. Only as a final step in the process will we overlay the events with the Gregorian day names so we can see the day of the week on which the events occur.

Learning the Jewish Mindset

To begin programming our minds to use the Jewish mindset of days, here are some examples of how days and times work in the Jewish culture.

- An evening begins at sunset and progresses until the moment before sunrise.
- A morning goes from sunrise and progresses until the moment before sunset.
- Since the day begins at sundown, the first meal of the day is supper, not breakfast.
- A day is comprised of an evening and a morning (Gen 1:5), which is different from a midnight to midnight western perception: the weekday that western culture observes as Thursday, July 21 goes from 00:00:00AM to 11:59:59PM in the Gregorian calendar; however, the day deemed as Thursday, July 21 in the Jewish calendar would go from sunset to sunset. Trying to understand the Jewish observation of "July 21" using the Gregorian calendar means the 21st begins at sunset on July 20 and goes till sunset on July 21 leaving the remainder of July 21 as part of July 22 on the Jewish calendar and leaving anything prior to sunset July 20 as part of July 19—draw this out on paper to help your understanding.
- A day is the summation of an evening and a morning irrespective of how they occur as long as they are in succession with each other—for more on this, pay special attention to the verse study on Gen 1:5. A slight western similarity might be to say that the period from 4PM one day to 4PM the next constitutes a day worth of time.
- In the Gregorian calendar, an hour is 60 minutes no matter the day of the year, but in the Jewish calendar, an hour[i] is defined as $1/12$ of the sunlight for that day, which changes based on

season—a Jerusalem hour in summer is longer than an hour in winter because the daylight lasts longer in the summer: consider an hour the movement of the shadow on a sundial by $1/12^{th}$ of the sundial arch. So, in April, the first hour would start at roughly 6:12AM[ii] as the sun rises. Each hour that day is roughly 65 minutes, so starting at 6:12 and adding 65 minutes for each notch on the sundial means the 9th hour of the day would be 9 notches on a sundial and would fall at roughly 2:45PM. North American locations on nearly the same latitude as Jerusalem are El Paso, TX or Ensenada on the Baja peninsula, 140 miles due south of San Diego.

- The Jewish month names in Scripture are different from the Gregorian names and there are more of them. For example, the first month of the Jewish calendar is currently named Nisan. It was also called Abib before the Jews were taken to the Babylonian exile, so you will observe Nisan and Abib as two names for the same month in Scripture.

- The Sabbath is not just a day of rest, it is a weekly feast of God with mandates on how it is to be celebrated, just like the remainder of God's feasts. So, when you read about Sabbath in this study, remember, the Sabbath is as much a feast as any other according to Leviticus 23:1-3.

These are just some of the basics and as you may guess, the Jewish calendar is quite involved and interwoven with their faith practice. Given these differences, trying to keep track of what Gregorian day holds a given Jewish event is best left as the last step of our process. We'll figure out all the relative days in the Passover and resurrection sequence first, then assign the day names at the end of the process. For us to record the sequence of events, we need some kind of naming convention that doesn't conflict with our existing 60-minute-12-month-365.25-day trained thought patterns, and I have just the method!

Creating Our Own Sequence for a Week

We must create our own day sequence to track the gospel account so that we don't get hung up on preconceived ideas. We aren't going to use names of days like Monday, Tuesday and Wednesday because they already have meaning to us. Instead, let's only use the Genesis idea of evening and morning. To succeed, our system has to distinguish between morning and evening, and needs to be scalar (1,2,3,4,5,6,7). To meet this task, let's use a function.

What is a Function?

If you use spreadsheet software or have basic algebra knowledge, you're already familiar with a function. It's a black box where you send in a value and it spits out some result. If you don't know what a function is, don't stop here. With a small amount of learning, it will make sense and you'll continue like a pro. Let's define a simple function with which you should already be familiar, and then we'll branch out to create our own.

Here is one you use every week when you pull up to a gas pump. You drive your vehicle into place, step out and look at the pump. The pump reads, $5/gallon. In your mind you think, "I need about five gallons" and immediately you use an equation to calculate the cost that will come out of your account: TotalCost = $5 x (the number of gallons I need). If I write that equation as a function, it looks like this: TotalCost(gallons) = $5 x gallons. Now to make this work, everywhere we see the word "gallons" we replace it with the number for which I want the calculation. TotalCost(5) = $5 * 5 would mean that if I send my function 5 for the number of gallons, it will return $25 for the cost. If I sent my function 10 gallons, it would look like this: TotalCost(10) = $5 x 10 and it would give me a total of $50. You do this mentally all the time, and a function is just a way of recording it. We send data in the parenthesis, it travels through the tunnel over to the other side of the equation, gets calculated and then the answer is passed back. I can invoke that function with any number I want, and it will always work. TotalCost(3) would give me $15; TotalCost(4) would give me $20; TotalCost(20) = $100; TotalCost(12) = $60, TotalCost(8) = $40. Is this starting to make sense? Once we have the equation set, we can use it whenever we want to give us the answer we need.

The nice thing about functions is that they become their own language, a kind of shorthand. For example, if I asked you what you'd get when you read: TotalCost(3), what would your answer be? If you said $15 you were right, because your brain did the math and you replied with the answer. If I said TotalCost(11) what would you reply? If you said $55, you'd have been right again. See, you learned how the function worked, and now you can communicate with it. We will do the same thing to track the chronology of the gospel accounts.

Creating Our Own Function

Let's use "e( )" to represent "evening," which is sunset to sunrise and "m( )" to represent "morning," which is sunrise to sunset. Doing this will help us remove the confusion of alternate meanings of "weekdays" so that we don't ask "now is this on Wednesday or Thursday?"

Next, let's put something in the parenthesis to establish some kind of sequence between all the e( )'s and m( )'s that we'll identify. Without something to identify a sequence, if we were to identify three different events on three different evenings that occurred between sunset and sunrise, it would mean our sequence would look like this e( ) e( ) e( ). We don't have enough information to know which e( ) comes before or after another. We really need something like e(1) e(2) and e(3) so that we have a way to know which comes first and so on.

Finally, for the purpose of this study, can we agree that "x" represents the day of Jesus' resurrection and the pivot point around which the gospel account revolves? We could choose any day, but the resurrection occurrence is the perfect anchor because we know specifically that the resurrection of Jesus happened before sunrise on the first day of the week (irrespective of a weekday name) because all four gospels tell us so. This allows us to say that the resurrection happened on e(x) which we pronounce "e of x" and which if we convert into our own language is read as the "evening of the resurrection" because the "e" means "evening" the ( )'s mean "of" and "x" means "the resurrection"—so, e(x) = the "evening of the resurrection" which is the time from sunset to before sunrise when the resurrection occurred. So, if I ask you what e(x) means, you reply, "the evening of the resurrection."

We've defined just three steps and now we have a system of tracking that has nothing to do with days of the week. And with a fixed, known time in the gospel narrative, specifically the resurrection or e(x) [again, pronounced "e of x"], we now have a way to go forward in time from the resurrection by adding a number inside the parenthesis or to go backward in time from the resurrection by subtracting a number inside the parenthesis. If we want to go to the next evening after the resurrection, we would write it as e(x+1) because we are going +1 evening forward and we would understand "e" = "evening", "( )" = "of", "x+1" = "the resurrection plus one" so it would be the "evening of the resurrection plus one" or in plain language "one evening after the resurrection." If we want to go two evenings past the resurrection, we write it as e(x+2) which equates to "e" = evening, "( )" = of, "x+2" = "the resurrection plus two" or "two evenings past the resurrection." If we want to go three evenings before the resurrection, we note it as e(x-3) [because we are subtracting days] which, when breaking it down, results in "e" = the evening, "( )" = of, "x-3" = "the resurrection minus three" making our result "three evenings before the resurrection." To go seven evenings before the resurrection would be e(x-7). To go three mornings before the resurrection would be m(x-3). To go 40 mornings after the resurrection would be m(x+40). Is this starting to make sense? So, if I ask you what is e(x-7), what is your reply? If you said, "seven evenings before the resurrection" you'd be correct! If I asked you what is m(x-6), what would be your reply? If you said "six mornings before the resurrection" you'd be correct again!

This is very important and key to understanding the gospel narrative, so before continuing, please do the activity titled, "Evening and Morning as Functions" in the appendices at the back. Become familiar with the idea of the function before you move forward, and you have my word, it will make your study pop. It's like turning on a headlamp in a dark cave.

Chapter End Notes/Observations

THE INVESTIGATION

As you investigate the following Scriptures, take time to digest their meaning and write down any questions you have. You're welcome to send questions to me, and I will help you figure out where in Scripture the response is found. You'll find my contact information at the end. I've worked diligently to disprove all that follows and cannot. To research something and believe it is true is one thing, but to do your best to disprove what you believe and to fail makes it all the more trustworthy. Do your best to prove and disprove your understandings. The Scripture is not at risk—it will defend itself.

Mise en Plus

In the kitchen, we have a term called "mise en plus" which means, "get all your ingredients ready before you start to cook!" Before you begin, get yourself a stack of paper, or even better, a stack of index cards. As you go through the Scriptures in this study, write them on cards and in the upper right corner of each card, write down the e( ) or m( ) notation so that when you're done, you can put them in date sequence. The goal is to let the Scripture narrative speak to us on its own. Having your own set of cards will help you understand more fully. At the end of each Scripture discussion, I state what I believe is that Scripture's relative position in the Passover and resurrection events. You can write that notation on the upper right corner of your card. If you disagree, flip the card over and write down why, then research to see if you can reconcile the differences. Feel free to contact me with questions: I'm glad to help.

Timeline Supports

As you read, you'll see timeline supports throughout the book. These are intended to help you understand the Scripture account you're exploring. Here is a copy of the first one you'll encounter. Let me explain it so that it makes sense when you encounter it, and others like it, moving forward.

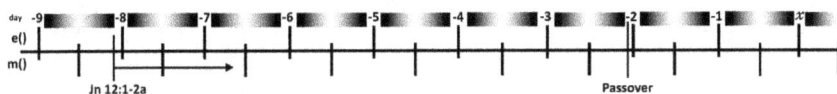

On the left, you'll note the e( ) and m( ) to signify "evening" and "morning": the evening is on top and the morning on bottom to remind you that the evening is the beginning of any given specific calendar day. The numbers going across the top are the relative day number (-9, -8, -7, etc.) in respect to the resurrection (x).

I've included a gradient block between the days to remind you that the day begins when the sun sets, moves through sunrise and back to sunset. If you examine the number -8 above, and if you look immediately to its right, you'll see the gradient moves from very dark to white and back to very dark signifying the time starting at evening, going to morning and then back to evening.

Finally, on the bottom, you'll find words highlighting important pieces of information. In the example here, you'll find Jn 12:1-2a and a vertical line, expressing that the events in that scripture began where the line extends upward into the day of x(-9) toward the end of that day, just before crossing over into e(x-8). The horizontal arrow also describes that the events progressed into e(x-7) showing the relative length of the account. You'll also note the word "Passover" in the example with a vertical line extending upward into the m(x-3) period. This shows the relative position of the Passover sacrifice on that given day.

Please take a few moments to study this example so that it makes sense. You'll experience this exact image again in a few moments, but there will be others throughout the study to help you in your investigation.

Spoiler Alert

I do need to offer one spoiler alert because it makes the rest of the study more fruitful. If we were to list the Scriptures the way they originally unraveled to show the chronology, the sequence would be difficult to follow. For weeks, I bounced all over the Scripture studying this and that, allowing my own intrigue to drive my reading. Because I believe it will be confusing without an early hint, I'd like us to agree on one assumption that you will see proven by the time we reach the end of the study: the relative position of the Passover celebration. A search with your favorite Internet search engine will show that this is a contested topic, but the Scripture is very plain about its occurrence when you read the full account of all four gospels as we will here. With this understanding, you will see the Passover celebration identified as $m(x-3)$ through the next pages. Recall that $m(x-3)$ just means "three mornings before the resurrection" and refers to the time of day spanning from sunrise to sunset. If you ask yourself, "How did he come to that assumption or conclusion?" You'll be able to authoritatively answer that question by the end.

Final Thoughts Before Beginning

Please read your Bible. This study isn't intended to replace the biblical text, it is intended to be open beside your biblical text. I only offer a small excerpt of each account. If you don't read the Scripture before reading my observations, this study will be impossible and unfruitful. You should read the Scriptures surrounding what I cite here and take your time to digest what you're reading. Find the Scripture I reference and read multiple verses in front and behind so that you seek the context. If the verse(s) appear in an account, read the entire account. Be curious and let your curiosity direct you. This isn't a race to get to the end, it's a treasure hunt with lots of excavations along the way. Where applicable, we will journey to the Old Testament to experience the foundations of the New Testament narrative. I use the King James for all referenced Scripture.

Finally, I've included a page at the end of each chapter titled "Chapter End Notes/Observations" so that you have a place to track thoughts, observations and questions. My hope is that you will keep these personal entries close to the biblical sources you're studying to fuel your train of thought.

With all these foundational issues out of the way, and with one more reminder of our functions, we will begin.

$e(x-3)$ = three evenings before the resurrection

$m(x+4)$ = four mornings after the resurrection

$m(x-7)$ = seven mornings before the resurrection

and...

$m(x-9)$ = nine mornings before the resurrection

Chapter End Notes/Observations

IN THE BEGINNING

Are you ready to go on the journey of your life? Let's pray, then we'll start. "God, I ask you to open my eyes to see the glorious story of planning, love and skilled execution that you've placed together in order to bring salvation to mankind. Please open my eyes to see the gospel accounts the way they happened and the way you intended. Holy Spirit, I ask you to teach me as Jesus said you would. I ask all this in Jesus' name. Amen."

Gen 1:5   **"...and the evening and the morning were the first day."**

The Jewish calendar is based on an evening and morning cycle. I'm intrigued by this language where the writer of Genesis includes the word "and" before "evening" and "morning" as it allows you to interchange their sequence. The phrase as written in Hebrew is "... and was evening and was morning...." (wayehi 'ereb wayehi boqer). This writing allows the morning and evening to be interchangeable such that when strung together in sequence, the chronology becomes "...and the morning and the evening and the morning and the evening." This presents a logically valid language structure and chronology describing that any successive combination of evening and morning can constitute a day: evening to evening would be a full day and morning to morning would be a full day. It should be noted, however, that for calendar days, the Jewish calendar runs evening to evening. This is a point worth understanding: calendar days go evening to evening, however, days as experienced may be any successive evening/morning combination. We discuss this in more detail later.

Jn 12:1-2a "Then Jesus six days before the Passover came to Bethany where Lazarus was which had been dead, whom he raised from the dead. There they made him a supper...."

Six days before the Passover feast begins, Jesus comes to Mary, Martha and Lazarus' house for dinner, and Mary anoints Jesus' feet for His burial. This appears to be on m(x-9) [nine mornings before the resurrection: after sunrise and before sunset] since the Passover meal begins at m(x-3) [three mornings before the resurrection] *just before* the sun sets (Ex 12:6) and Jesus' supper with Mary, Martha and Lazarus would have been at a similar time of day.

The sequence, then, seems to be: Jesus arrived at Mary, Martha and Lazarus' house on m(x-9) before sunset, supper began as the first meal of the day on e(x-8) [because m(x-9) is before e(x-8) in the evening to evening day] and Jesus spent the evening enjoying the dinner with His friends. This continued until an unknown ending time that night or later. This event appears to start toward the end of m(x-9).

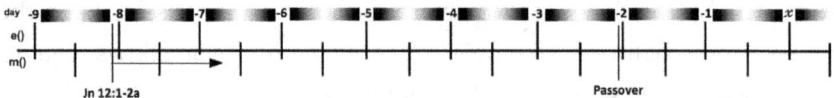

Now, write this Scripture on your page or card and put "m(x-9)" in the upper right corner for later use.

Jn 12:12-13 "On the next day much people that were come to the feast, when they heard that Jesus was coming to Jerusalem [13] Took branches of palm trees, and went forth to meet him, and cried, Hosanna: Blessed [is] the King of Israel that cometh in the name of the Lord."

If you haven't already, read this full account as written by John and then return here to continue. In our attempt to understand these two passages (Jn 12:1-2a and Jn 12:12-13), at a minimum, we should read Jn 12:1-19, because this offers us ample background as we move into the Scriptures we're evaluating, and it also takes us to the next change of thought. This is what we look for as we study: a complete scriptural account with enough backstory to understand what we are investigating; continuing all the way until the scene changes away from where we started. Think of it like watching a movie. You'd never expect to enter the middle of a movie and fully understand its plot, that would be laughable. Often, when we try to study Scripture, we make our goal finding an outcome or an application and then moving on. Our flesh wants to get in and get out, but learning and understanding takes investment and patience: it is a spiritual discipline. Take the time necessary to read all you need; let natural curiosity feed your reading: it's worth it! Let's continue.

"On the next day," people went to meet Jesus with palm branches and ushered Him into the city, but on the next day from what? "The next day" from His time at Mary, Martha and Lazarus' house. The account, then, is: Jesus comes before supper on m(x-9); He eats supper with Mary, Martha and Lazarus on e(x-8); He is anointed by Mary that evening and at some point the supper ends after sunset, which puts the end of the meal sometime in e(x-8) [after sunset and before sunrise] or m(x-8) if the meal went all night long.

Jesus was evidently at the Mary, Martha and Lazarus' dwelling for a period of time because people came to visit him, to listen to him teach, to see Lazarus who was raised from the dead; and, the pharisees also had time to meet and contrive (Jn 12:9-11). The "next day" after this would begin at e(x-7) in an evening-to-evening calendar. Since Jesus entry into Jerusalem happened during daylight, this would have to be m(x-7) since that is after sunrise on the next day.

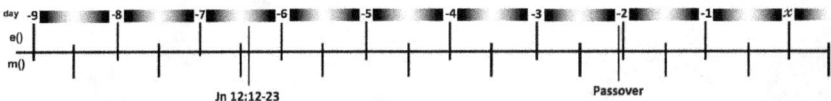

17

This event, when Jesus enters Jerusalem, occurred four days before the Passover feast. Since the Passover feast happens on the 14th day of the month (Ex. 12:6), that makes this the 10th day of the month. This is a significant day in the Scripture account as it relates to the Passover. On the 10th day of the first month, throughout the entire nation of Israel, each individual home is ushering in its Passover lamb where it will dwell with them until it is sacrificed (Ex. 12:3-11). Ironically, Jesus is ushered into the house of Israel by the same people at the same time where He will dwell with them until His sacrifice.

Write the Jn 12:12-13 Scripture on your page or card and put m(x-7) in the upper right corner. From this point forward, you're on your own. Just remember to write each Scripture on your page or card and to put the e( ) or m( ) notation in the upper right corner so you'll have all you need at the end of the study to arrange the Scripture in chronological order to see the events unfold for yourself.

Chapter End Notes/Observations

WHAT'S IN A FEAST?

Very few people enjoy reading a dictionary. We could have read through all the key terms at the beginning of the book so that you would be familiar with them before needing them, but I was hedging on the fact that you'd skip that section, so instead, we'll define key terms as we encounter them. Here, I'm separating the first two terms and their definitions into their own chapter because they are extensive, but moving forward, you'll see terms defined in-line, right with the Scripture verses they support. Here are two very important definitions to understand before moving forward in your study.

Feasts **Celebrations divinely established and mandated by God, all of which are prophetic to foretell Jesus' ministry and person and all of which are required celebrations for the nation of Israel. Each feast has obligations and restrictions for work and worship and sometimes for food as well.**

The seven mandated feasts of God are found in Leviticus 23:
1. the Sabbath feast which occurs weekly beginning as the sun sets on the sixth day of the week ushering in the seventh and final day of the week and which continues until the sun sets on the seventh day of the week ushering in the first day of a new week—this is not just a time of rest, it is a full feast each week;

2. the feast of Unleavened Bread that begins with the Passover meal on the 15th day of the first month (Nisan), where just prior to this as the sun is setting on the 14th day of the month, the Passover lamb is sacrificed for each family in Israel;

3. the feast of First Fruits that happens with the first harvest of the new year, often happening during the feast of Unleavened Bread in the first month (Nisan) of the year;

4. the feast of Pentecost that happens in the third month (the month of Sivan), seven weeks (actually 50 days) after the feast of the First Fruits begins—literally, the feast of the First Fruits launches the countdown to the feast of Pentecost, which is the celebration of the second harvest;

5. the feast of Trumpets which happens on the first day of the seventh month (Tishri);

6. the feast of Atonement which happens on the 10th day of the seventh month (Tishri); and

7. the feast of Tabernacles which goes from the 15th to the 22nd day of the seventh month (Tishri).

Many sources separate the Passover sacrifice on the 14th as a separate feast, however, this is not biblical. Also, Leviticus 23 very specifically notes that the first feast is a *weekly* feast called the Sabbath. Confusion comes when people read how the writer of Exodus repeats part of the instruction in verse four, "These *are* the feasts of the LORD, *even* holy convocations," then adds "which ye shall proclaim in their seasons." It appears that individuals interpret the weekly Sabbath feast differently since verse four repeats the instruction from verse two that those events after verse four are feasts as well. However, note the defining difference between the Sabbath feast and the other feasts. In Leviticus 23:2, God says, "...these are my feasts." He then states the weekly Sabbath feast. In verse four He then changes to feast that are *not* weekly, and adds "...which ye shall proclaim in their seasons." These seven are all feasts, its merely that the Sabbath feast happens weekly, and the remainder of the feasts happen "…in their seasons." Verses two and four should not bring confusion, but clarified understanding. This is a very important piece to understand the Passover celebration, because on the year Jesus is crucified the Sabbath Feast, with all of its requirements, was observed with the Passover and affects what the Jewish people could do at His death and burial.

This study does not cover all the feasts: we will only touch the first two. But you should realize that Jesus and His ministry are visible all through the feasts. In short order, if you consider Jesus' fulfilling all the feasts of God, you have Him as: our regular rest and celebration; our sinless sacrifice of atonement; the first-fruits from the dead; the baptizer in the Holy Spirit; the returning King at the last trumpet; our atonement to God and the final restorer of the atoned to live eternally with God. Every year, for the past nearly 3,500 years the Jewish nation has celebrated the feasts of God in anticipation and expectation of His final redemption and the fulfillment of His promises. The feasts are prophetic and pervasive, and our basic understanding is necessary.

Passover	**The first feast of the new Jewish year that commemorates the deliverance of God from bondage through the sacrifice of a lamb, the shedding of blood for forgiveness of sin, the application of blood on the doorposts of each home, the removal of sin from each dwelling and God honoring His word that the angel of death would pass over each dwelling having the blood of the atoning sacrifice applied to it.**

This Greek word for "Passover" can mean: the sacrificial lamb itself, the first meal of the feast of Unleavened Bread, or the entire Feast of Unleavened Bread. In the Greek, the same word is used to represent all three so context is the only way we can know which is being referenced.

The Passover begins at sunset on the 14th day with the sacrifice of the Passover lamb just before dusk and moves seamlessly into the first meal of the day on the evening of the 15th of Nisan as the nation celebrates the Feast of Unleavened Bread.

The Passover is pivotal in the gospel accounts we are about to read, so let's take a few moments to learn about it before continuing.

The feast begins with the lamb being sacrificed before sunset on the 14th day of the first month, after which, a feast commences at the beginning of (sunset) the 15th day of the first month and lasts seven days, ending on the 21st day of the same month. This feast is mandated for the entire nation of Israel, and if an Israelite does not keep the Passover sacrifice and the Feast of Unleavened Bread according to the law of God, that person is to be removed from the nation of Israel.

The feast of Unleavened Bread is a very important feast where everyone participating, priest or otherwise, is expected to cleanse their selves and to make their person and their dwelling clean from sin and presentable to God according to the Law of Moses and before participating.

Ex 12:6   **"And ye shall keep it [the Passover sacrificial lamb] up until the fourteenth day of the same month: and the whole assembly of the congregation of Israel shall kill it in the evening."**

From the 10th day m(x-7) of the month of Nisan to the 14th day m(x-3) of the month, the Passover lamb was kept at each home of Israel until "…the whole assembly will kill it in the evening." Evening is generally defined as the time at the end of the day, right before sunset. Here is the section of Scripture explaining this (Ex 12:3-11):

> ³ Speak ye unto all the congregation of Israel, saying, In the tenth [day] of this month they shall take to them every man a lamb, according to the house of [their] fathers, a lamb for an house: ⁴ And if the household be too little for the lamb, let him and his neighbour next unto his house take [it] according to the number of the souls; every man according to his

eating shall make your count for the lamb. [5] Your lamb shall be without blemish, a male of the first year: ye shall take [it] out from the sheep, or from the goats: [6] And ye shall keep it up until the fourteenth day of the same month: and the whole assembly of the congregation of Israel shall kill it in the evening. [7] And they shall take of the blood, and strike [it] on the two side posts and on the upper door post of the houses, wherein they shall eat it. [8] And they shall eat the flesh in that night, roast with fire, and unleavened bread; [and] with bitter [herbs] they shall eat it. [9] Eat not of it raw, nor sodden at all with water, but roast [with] fire; his head with his legs, and with the purtenance thereof. [10] And ye shall let nothing of it remain until the morning; and that which remaineth of it until the morning ye shall burn with fire. [11] And thus shall ye eat it; [with] your loins girded, your shoes on your feet, and your staff in your hand; and ye shall eat it in haste: it [is] the LORD'S passover.

With this scriptural understanding of the Passover, let's return to our study of the Gospel accounts and watch for these pieces as we journey with Jesus through the final hours of His life.

Chapter End Notes/Observations

WHAT HAPPENED NEXT?

W e previously began with John's account of Jesus entering Jerusalem, now let's look at Matthew's account of the same event.

Mt 20:18-21:9   **"Behold, we go up to Jerusalem; and the Son of man shall be betrayed unto the chief priests and unto the scribes and they shall condemn him to death,"**

Continuing…

> [19] And shall deliver him to the Gentiles to mock, and to scourge, and to crucify [him]: and the third day he shall rise again…[21:8] And a very great multitude spread their garments in the way; others cut down branches from the trees, and strawed [them] in the way. [9] And the multitudes that went before, and that followed, cried, saying, Hosanna to the Son of David: Blessed [is] he that cometh in the name of the Lord; Hosanna in the highest.

Matthew's account of Jesus' entry into Jerusalem is prefixed with Jesus telling the disciples what would happen to Him after arriving. While Matthew doesn't give enough data to create a relative date for this event, we know that Jesus and the disciples were on their way from Jericho to Jerusalem (Mt 20:29) and when they reached the Mount of Olives, Jesus sent the disciples to get a colt for Him to ride. Matthew doesn't offer any defining days or times in his narrative, so if we want one, we have to rely on John's gospel. In John's gospel we have this as four days before the Passover making this m(x-7). Let's use that date and continue studying. If something disagrees with this later, we'll circle back and change it.

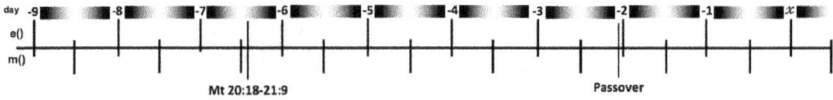

Mt 20:18-21:9   Passover

Note in Matthew, we see a reference to one of the "third day" Scriptures. Jesus uses many references to three and third when referencing His resurrection, perhaps the most defining being Jesus' self-identification with the prophet Jonah.

Mt 12:40   **"For as Jonas was three days and three nights in the whale's belly; so shall the Son of man be three days and three nights in the heart of the earth."**

This Scripture is a key prophetic verse from Jesus that gives a specific timeline for the resurrection. There is much more in Jesus' reference to this prophecy than just the amount of time He will be in the grave. The prophecy is an account of much that Jesus will experience beside death and resurrection.

Jesus specifically states a historical chronology: Jonah was three days and three nights in the fish's belly. Jesus notes that Jonah's event chronology starts on a day, goes into a night and repeats for two more iterations. Then, Jesus identifies that His chronology will be identical: He will enter "the heart of the earth" during a day, be there a night, and repeat this for two more days.

Jesus was referencing this section of Scripture in Jonah chapter 2:

> [1] Then Jonah prayed unto the LORD his God out of the fish's belly, [2] And said, I cried by reason of mine affliction unto the LORD, and he heard me; out of the belly of hell cried I, [and] thou heardest my voice. [3] For thou hadst cast me into the deep, in the midst of the seas; and the floods compassed me about: all thy billows and thy waves passed over me. [4] Then I said, I am cast out of thy sight; yet I will

27

look again toward thy holy temple. [5] The waters compassed me about, [even] to the soul: the depth closed me round about, the weeds were wrapped about my head. [6] I went down to the bottoms of the mountains; the earth with her bars [was] about me for ever: yet hast thou brought up my life from corruption, O LORD my God. [7] When my soul fainted within me I remembered the LORD: and my prayer came in unto thee, into thine holy temple. [8] They that observe lying vanities forsake their own mercy. [9] But I will sacrifice unto thee with the voice of thanksgiving; I will pay [that] that I have vowed. Salvation [is] of the LORD. [10] And the LORD spake unto the fish, and it vomited out Jonah upon the dry [land].

A number of crucifixion and resurrection parallels are noteworthy. In rapid-fire format, consider the following: v2. "out of the belly of hell I cried" noting Jesus descended to the "lower earthly regions" (Eph 4:9); v3. the term "waves" is also used in Hebrew to represent piles of stone over a dead body; v4. allusion to coming out of hell to once again enter the temple, points to His resurrection and entering the Holiest of holies in God's presence; v5. He states He will die, and His head will be "wrapped about" which alludes to the head cloth described in Jn 20:6-7[iii]; v6. Jesus is placed under the earth, under a hill and again will be raised from the dead, which agrees with the prophecy that His body would not see destruction [Ps 16:10, Acts 2:31, 13:37]; v8. seems to agree with the rest of Mt 12 where Jesus is warning of Israel rejecting him and their later state being worse than their former; v9. seems to be a tie back to the prophecy Paul references in Hebrews 10:5-7 that comes from Ps. 40:7-8 where Jesus at some point agreed with His Father to become man and take on His mission, ultimately journeying to the Holiest of Holies in the presence of God to fulfill His vow to God; v10. God speaking to the fish so it would vomit Jonah was synonymous with God forcing the grave to give up Jesus.

The Jonah chapter two reference that Jesus makes points to more than just His time in the grave, but also to the chronology and specifics of His death, burial, grave experience and time till resurrection. While we don't know the date that Jesus spoke Mt 12:40 itself, the beginning of the three days and three nights that Jesus discusses would be m(x-3) because Scripture accounts that Jesus was absent from the grave before m(x), meaning the three m( )'s Jesus was in the grave were m(x-3), m(x-2) and m(x-1) because before reaching m(x) He was already resurrected. This is the most definitive place we see the m(x-3) defining Jesus time of death.

While we're in Matthew's gospel, consider what this Gospel writer describes as happening, possibly the next evening.

Mt 26: 1-2   **"And it came to pass, when Jesus had finished all these sayings, he said unto his disciples, 2 Ye know that after two days is the passover, and the Son of man is betrayed to be crucified."**

Jesus stated, "…after two days is the feast of the Passover…." Reading the chronology in Matthew shows the following day transitions: Mt 21 Jesus enters Jerusalem on the colt, which according to John's gospel was the 10th day of the month (Nisan) and that night He goes to Bethany to lodge (Mt 21:17); the next day (Nisan 11) toward the end of the day, Jesus goes to the Mount of Olives (Mt 24:3) and when Jesus finishes teaching there (Mt 26:2) He says "after two days is the Passover" and, by this point, it is either late in the day of the 11th or early evening on the 12th. So, Jesus saying "after two days is the Passover" is accurate since the evening of the 14th of the first month (Nisan) is the Passover sacrifice. This is one of the scriptures that points to the Passover possibly being at the end of m(x-3): for the Passover to be two days after this account in Mt 26:1-2, it would make this verse happen sometime at the end of m(x-6) or the beginning of e(x-5). We continue to watch for clarity as we read other accounts.

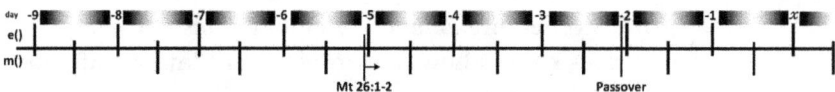

Mt 26:3-5   "Then assembled together the chief priests, and the scribes, and the elders of the people, unto the palace of the high priest, who was called Caiaphas, ⁴ And consulted that they might take Jesus by subtilty, and kill [him]. ⁵ But they said, Not on the feast, lest there be an uproar among the people."

At the same time the previous Scriptures happen in Mt 26:1-2, the chief priests, scribes and elders meet at the palace of the high priest, Caiaphas, to conspire Jesus' death and determine that He will be executed, but "not on the feast." This account ultimately leads to Judas helping them in vv. 14-16. Note that Judas is not yet involved at this point. Matthew does not give a specific date, but given the chronology, it seems this is e(x-5) or m(x-5). We can't be certain from Matthew's account if Jesus was going to Bethany (v. 6) or not, so we must leave this verse as a guess and try to fill it in from other gospels as we progress.

Mt 26:6   "Now when Jesus was in Bethany, in the house of Simon the leper"

This comes just after v.2, which records Jesus stating that after two days was the Passover, but doesn't give how far from that sentence to this account has passed: it only says "...as he sat at meat." So, we know it was at least two days before Passover because of verse 6, but given that we're missing specifics before landing on verse 17, we don't know if the meal at Simon the leper's house was lunch or supper which would define the day. Given this ambiguity, we do know it would have been at least m(x-5), but we're still left a bit in the dark as to if it was later, perhaps even e(x-4).

Gratefully, Mark offers details in his account to fill in the gaps to help us eliminate one piece of the puzzle.

Mk 14:1-3   "After two days was [the feast of] the passover, and of unleavened bread: and the chief priests and the scribes sought how they might take him by craft, and put [him] to death."

Continuing...

> [2] But they said, Not on the feast [day], lest there be
> an uproar of the people. [3] And being in Bethany in
> the house of Simon the leper, as he sat at meat, there
> came a woman having an alabaster box of ointment
> of spikenard very precious; and she brake the box,
> and poured [it] on his head.

The Passover was at the end of m(x-3) toward evening, so to be "after two days," this account would have been sometime before the 9th hour (when the Passover lamb sacrifices began). That makes this m(x-5) and possibly as early as e(x-5) when the chief priests convened. We know it was not later because Mark's account identifies that Jesus was at Simon the Leper's house already (v. 3) when the chief priests and scribes convened, meaning they had to arrive together before or at a minimum, simultaneously with Jesus as He arrived to Simon's dwelling.

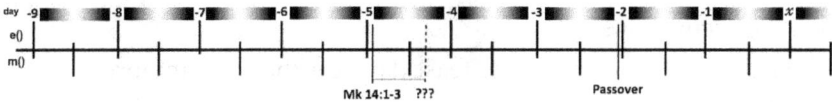

More observations show Mark noting that after two days was the Passover sacrifice and then he identifies the feast, signifying that neither had yet happened, so we know this event wasn't somehow during the feast itself. Also note that Judas is not yet involved with the Jewish conspirators at the time of this meal at Simon's house.

Here then is the first place we see the m(x-3) Passover substantiated. We have already learned that Jesus must die on m(x-3) to fulfill the prophecy of Jonah. We see here at Simon's house that Jesus is not yet dead. We see that these events happened two days before the Passover lamb sacrifice. At a minimum, this must be two days before Jesus death, because Jesus would not be killed by the Jewish leaders during the feast. This means that if the Jewish leaders are going to kill Jesus, they only have the next two days to do it if they intend to meet their own self-imposed deadline. Two days after m(x-5) would be m(x-3) before the Passover lambs are killed at sunset. To be successful, the Jewish leaders must kill Jesus before the sun sets, two days hence on m(x-3). Remember, according to the Jonah prophecy, Jesus dies on m(x-3) as well, so we have the convergence of two different plans: one from the Jewish leaders to kill Jesus before the feast, and one from the Jonah prophecy; each pointing to m(x-3).

Here are a few more observations from this rich area of Scripture. The insertion of the phrase "…and of unleavened bread" had to mean "the feast after the Passover sacrifice" because the Feast of Unleavened Bread was actually the day *after* the Passover sacrifice, happening annually on the 15th day of the first month (Nisan). The only way an observer could recognize the sacrifice and the feast as happening on the same day would be to reference this time period as a gentile observer with the Roman calendar, in which case it's the same 24-hour period from midnight to midnight, because Nisan 14 after sunrise and Nisan 15 at sunset are the same Roman "24 hour" day. Either way, the chronology of the events as mandated by God would be sacrifice on the 14th followed by meal on the 15th and we know that neither occurred yet.

The phrase "…not on the feast day, lest there be an uproar of the people…" would mean one of two things: a) these leaders decided their plan would not be executed during the 15th to the 21st days of the first month [from e(x-2) through e(x+4)], since those were the dates for the Feast of Unleavened Bread each year; or b) their plan would not be carried out between e(x-2) and e(x-1) which would be the first Passover feast day when the lamb was roasted and consumed by each family in Israel. Either way, the accounts agree that, at a minimum, the Jewish leaders were determined not to arrest Jesus on e(x-2) which is pivotal for understanding the events that follow.

Notable is that this is now the second time Jesus was anointed by a woman for His burial. The first time was e(x-9) at Mary, Martha and Lazarus' house where His feet were anointed by Mary and where she wiped His feet dry with her hair. Now at e(x-5) it happens a second time at a different location and this time it's His head (Jn 12:11; Mt 26:6-13; Mk 14:3). This is significant because Jesus explains in both cases that it is for His burial, a prophetic response that He would not be properly interred, because, as we know in hindsight, He would not be in the grave when the ladies returned to prepare Him properly for His burial. The disciples didn't catch this allusion.

Mk 14:3,10-11 **"And being in Bethany in the house of Simon the leper, as he sat at meat, there came a woman having an alabaster box of ointment of spikenard very precious;"**

Continuing...

> and she brake the box, and poured it on his head...[10] And Judas Iscariot, one of the twelve, went unto the chief priests, to betray him unto them. [11] And when they heard [it], they were glad, and promised to give him money. And he sought how he might conveniently betray him.

Judas goes to the Jewish leaders and agrees to betray Jesus for money. We don't know if the meal at Simon's house was lunch or supper because the Greek words used are not descriptive enough to tell us, but if it was lunch, Judas would have gone on m(x-5) or by that point e(x-4).

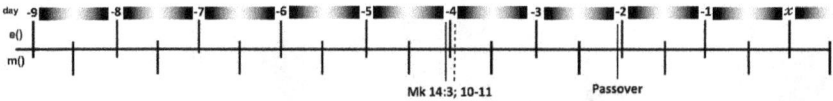

Here, then, is a timeline of all we've examined so far:

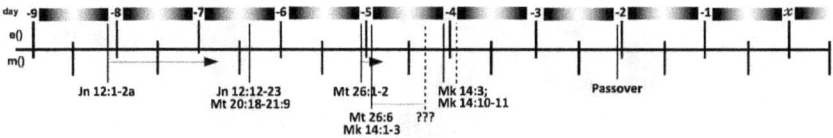

The historical record that goes with this timeline is as follows: six days before the Passover sacrifice, Jesus goes to eat dinner at Mary, Martha and Lazarus' house where He is anointed for His burial (Jn

12:1-2a); Jesus stays a period of time; four days before, He enters Jerusalem (Jn 12:12-23; Mt 20:18-21:9); two days before, the priests and scribes begin to plot Jesus' death (Mt 26:3; Mk 14:1-3); the same day He is at Simon the Leper's house where He is anointed for His burial a second time (Mt 26:6; Mk 14:3); later that day or early evening the next day, Judas leaves the meal at Simon's and approaches the Jewish leaders, joining forces to betray Him (Mk 14:10-11). The Jewish leaders have now dedicated their selves to eliminate Jesus before the Feast of Unleavened Bread which is only two days away.

Chapter End Notes/Observations

PREPARING FOR THE PASSOVER SACRIFICE

As we transition to the Passover sacrifice preparations, consider this verse in Deuteronomy that makes the point to limit where this Passover celebration can happen.

Deut 16:5-6   **"Thou mayest not sacrifice the passover within any of thy gates, which the LORD thy God giveth thee: 6 But at the place which the LORD thy God shall choose to place his name in, there thou shalt sacrifice the passover at even, at the going down of the sun, at the season that thou camest forth out of Egypt."**

God only allowed specific places for the Passover sacrifice. It must be the place where God has set His Name, and that would have been Jerusalem. Passover sacrifices had to be offered at Jerusalem, at a minimum.

Deuteronomy 12:11 states:

> Then there shall be a place which the LORD your God shall choose to cause his name to dwell there; thither shall ye bring all that I command you; your burnt offerings, and your sacrifices, your tithes, and the heave offering of your hand, and all your choice vows which ye vow unto the LORD....

In 1Kings 8:28-29, Solomon invites God to dwell in the temple of Jerusalem and God replies in 1Kings 9:1-3, saying:

> And it came to pass, when Solomon had finished the building of the house of the LORD, and the king's house, and all Solomon's desire which he was pleased to do, That the LORD appeared to Solomon the second time, as he had appeared unto him at Gibeon. And the LORD said unto him, I have heard thy prayer and thy supplication, that thou hast made before me: I have hallowed this house, which thou hast built, to put my name there for ever; and mine eyes and mine heart shall be there perpetually.

It is unclear if God ever chose any other place to place His name for the Passover sacrifice, but we know definitively that Jerusalem met the requirements, and Jerusalem is the setting for the account we are examining right now.

As we enter the following sections of Scripture, please take your time to read and discern them. The Scriptures we are about to experience took quite a lot of time to dissect because the translation of the original Greek wording was constructed around the translators' apparent Friday to Sunday bias, however, the Scriptures theirselves don't state this timeline. Let's continue with a key term:

Prepare   The Greek work for "prepare" or "preparation" (παρασκευή) is used six times, all in the gospels. It refers to the process of getting ready for a feast.

Matthew, Mark and Luke all use this word once and John does three times. The same word is used in preparation for the Sabbath as well as for a feast because the Sabbath is a feast of God (Lev 23:1-3). Context is the only way to know which is referenced, so if two feast days are next to each other or on the same day, knowing which preparation is being referenced can only happen as a byproduct of context and comparison, if at all. This is the hurdle we must jump in our study of Jesus' crucifixion and His Passover celebration.

Mk 14:12   **"And the first day of unleavened bread, when they killed the passover, his disciples said unto him, Where wilt thou that we go and prepare that thou mayest eat the passover?"**

Here, we first examine the phrase "and the first day of unleavened bread, when they killed the passover…." Understanding this verse in light of the rest of Mark's gospel is the only way to see what he intends because at first glance there are seeming inconsistencies. To begin, the first day of unleavened bread is Nisan 15 and not Nisan 14 when the Passover lamb is killed. Mark reversing them may be a literary move based on the possibility that he is writing to an audience that would see both events as happening in the same day since they both happen in the evening of a midnight to midnight time frame. However, as it is written, this verse does not support a literal chronology because the order is reversed: it should be "when they killed the passover" and then the first day of Unleavened Bread. It appears, then, that "when they killed the passover" is intended to modify "And the first of unleavened bread" as a clarifying point to the readers, not an attempt at chronology.

Also, this cannot be the first day of the Feast of Unleavened Bread because of 1) the determination of the Jewish leaders that Mark explains in Mk 14:1-2; and 2) the unfolding events of the crucifixion that would not happen on the literal "first" day as in "the first day of the Feast of Unleavened Bread" on Nisan 15. The priests were dedicated against any activities that would cause an uproar at the feast.

Since it is night from Mk 14:17 until Mk 15:1, this also suggests we should not interpret this day as "the preparation" day that is often the immediate day before the Feast of Unleavened Bread when the Passover lamb itself is sacrificed at nightfall, since if it were, the accounts after this one in Mk 15 (Jesus' trial before the Sanhedrin) and forward would then land on the first day of the Feast of Unleavened

Bread; again, something the Jewish leaders did not want and couldn't do without breaking God's law for work restrictions on the first day of the Passover feast.

So, Mark supports the disciple's preparation for the Passover a day before another preparation because Mk 15:42 notes that the crucifixion day was preparation "before the Sabbath...."

The key to unlock Mk 14:12 is in Mk 15:42 and is the word "day" in the phrase "day before the Sabbath." This word "day" is not in the Greek, but is only identified by the interpreters as part of the word in their translation. The problem arises because (προσάββατον – prosabbaton) as written only means "before Sabbath" not "day before the Sabbath" and contains no ordinal position associated with it (this is discussed in more detail later). So preparation for Passover here in Mk 14:12 is believable and possible if this first referenced preparation was Passover preparation that was earlier for the disciples than other people in Israel, and where the later preparations in Mk 15:42 are for other's observed Passover meal, for a Sabbath happening during or immediately after the Passover meal, or both. In any interpretation, the Greek word (προσάββατον – prosabbaton) by itself doesn't tell us the span of time between the preparation day and the celebration day, which is very important to us.

We find another piece of the puzzle is the definition of the word "first" in Mk 14:12. Consider the following observations while examining this section of Scripture:

- The Greek word for "first" is protos which also determines "first in succession" not just "the absolute day before a pre-determined other." For example, protos works in the phrase, "the first day before my birthday" where my birthday is a date on the calendar. It also works when stating, "the first day of the winter Olympics" where it expresses the beginning of a sequence, but where the planners may not have yet chosen a date. In the first example, we know a pivotal date and the word protos takes on a specific definition based on the antecedent. In the second example, we don't know the days, we just know their occurrence order begins with the protos (first day) and continues on for some length after that. We may not even know how many days the Olympics may last, and yet we know we are discussing the first day of that range. Finally, the word "first" also works in "the first day we prepare for a birthday party" because it signifies the first of possibly many days before a calendar event with no sense of how long between the start of the preparation and the actual date of the event. If the event was the 22nd of the month, we could prepare on three different days: the 12th, the 15th and 20th. The 12th in that example is the first day (protos) of preparation for the event on the 22nd.

- The phrase "when they killed the Passover" appears to be a clarification of the celebration, and not necessarily defining the actual day itself, since these are two different days on the Jewish calendar (Nisan 14 and Nisan 15). Both are referenced in this verse and they are in reverse order with the Passover celebration being referenced before the Passover sacrifice.

- "where wilt thou that we go and prepare?" confirms it was a day of preparation for the disciples (whether it was for anyone else or not). The reason they would observe a separate preparation day is not covered in the Scripture, but it is covered in the Mishnah (part of the Jewish laws and history) and is discussed later. For now, we just know that the disciples did a day of preparation before the rest of Israel and this observation is validated through the other gospels.

- In Mk 14:14, "where I shall eat" seems to be translated either by bias or conjecture as the words Jesus speaks are in the aorist tense subjunctive mood and active voice, meaning "where I may or may not eat." The aorist tense means it was a simple one-time action; the subjunctive mood means it is unclear if it will occur and where there is a level of doubt; and the active voice means Jesus is doing the action rather than being acted upon. Jesus never says He will eat the Passover, instead He says where it may or may not happen. In the disciples' case, they did eat the Passover meal; in Jesus' case...He did not eat the actual Passover meal itself as we will see shortly. Noteworthy, however, is that Jesus did partake some of the

"Passover" feast (aka/ the Feast of Unleavened Bread) when He appears to the disciples three days later in the upper room and consumes fish and some honeycomb to show them He was not a ghost (Lk 24:42). So, we see Jesus' response of "may or may not" is a truthful representation, that while He did not eat the Passover meal with the disciples as the first meal of the Feast of Unleavened Bread, He did later eat with them during the Feast of Unleavened Bread.

- If you read the events from Mk 14:40-15:6, you will note that we have still not reached the feast day.

It appears that Mark is making a statement in Mk 14:12 that reads like this: "And the first [in a sequence] day of unleavened bread, [recognized as the time] when they [the Jewish people] killed the Passover [sacrifice], His disciples said…."

Mark is noting the sequence of days has begun and is only clarifying to the reader that this sequence includes when the Passover lamb is offered. Further, the sequence follows this pattern: the Passover is at hand; the disciples ask about preparations; Jesus sends two of them to the upper room to prepare; the two go and prepare for the Passover meal; Jesus and the others join later; they eat together [it is conjecture to assume they eat the Passover meal because preparations occurred]; they go to Gethsemane; Jesus is arrested that night; the next morning he's tried; He gives up the ghost; there was another preparation identified as (προσάββατον – prosabbaton – the word gives no definition to how many days before the Sabbath the preparation occurs); then the Sabbath passes (Mk 16:1).

In the narrative, the only way we can make the assumption that this is the immediate day before the Passover feast is based on the few places one can find the use of (προσάββατον – prosabbaton) in extra-biblical texts. This word is only used once in the Scripture and sparingly in other searchable Greek resources. While this is discussed later in more detail, the take-away here is that given the sequence of events, this event in Mk 14:12 with Jesus and the disciples preparing for their Passover feast seems obvious as the day before the actual sacrifice of the Passover lamb and subsequent first day of Unleavened Bread, since the two events are hours apart. That would make this verse of Mk 14:12 the morning period [after sunrise and before sunset] before the Passover sacrifice that happened at the end of m(x-3) making this occurrence m(x-4).

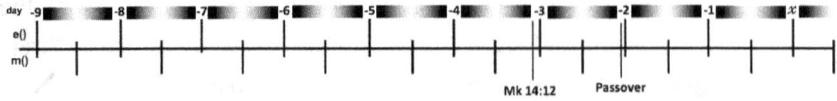

| Mt 26:17 | "Now the first [day] of the [feast of] unleavened bread the disciples came to Jesus, saying unto him, Where wilt thou that we prepare for thee to eat the passover?" |

As we just discussed from Mark's gospel, so here in Matthew's account, the word "day" is not in the Greek. Also, Matthew does not show he believes this was the first day of the feast in his own account because all prep would be done before this day, not on this day, since the first day of the feast is Nisan 15 and the Passover lamb would have been sacrificed on Nisan 14 at evening which launches the feast; all preparations must be done *by then*. To believe the inserted word "day" references an ordinal position that places it on Nisan 14 is conjecture or bias because the sentence itself, even as translated, is not accurate with the Jewish practice. This assumption also goes against Matthew's continuing narrative in Mt 26:3-5 where Matthew identifies that the Jews did not want to make an uproar on the feast day since if this were the actual preparation the day before the feast, that would make Jesus arrest and trial on the first day of the feast itself.

Matthew 27:1 states "When the morning [after the disciples preparation] was come, all the chief priests and elders of the people took counsel against Jesus to put him to death…" which, if Mt 26:17 references Nisan 14, would have made the Chief Priests and elders seek to kill Jesus on the first day of the Feast of Unleavened Bread on Nisan 15, a day on which the priest and leaders were disallowed from working and the day away from which the leaders wanted to stay so that an uproar didn't begin when they did kill Jesus.

Also, the fact that Mt 27:62 states "Now the next day, that followed the day of the preparation, the chief priests and Pharisees came together unto Pilate," could not be a Sabbath (i.e. if Jesus was crucified on a Friday before sunset) because the priests could not have worked on the Sabbath day and would not have gone to Pilate on the Sabbath day since they were restricted by the law of Moses from all work and each man is told to "stay in his place" (cf. Ex. 16:29). So, the day of preparation on which Jesus was crucified could not have been the Sabbath preparation as the immediate day before the Sabbath since no work of any kind is allowed on the Sabbath and people are expected to stay in their dwellings (Ex 12:16).

What we observe then is the following narrative from Mt 26:17-28:1: now the first [in succession] of the unleavened bread (with no use of the word "day" in Scripture) the disciples prepare; they eat together; leave the upper room to which they will again return later in the narrative; go to Gethsemane; Jesus is arrested; Jesus is crucified and that day was the preparation (for others in Israel); the day after this preparation, the priests and rulers are able to leave their homes, go to the Roman ruler because the Sabbath feast and day of rest has not yet commenced; the leaders talk with the Romans, travel to the tomb and watch as a guard is posted and the tomb sealed; then the Sabbath comes and expires (Mt 28:1).

Review the chapter "What's in a Feast" if necessary, then recognize the only way this narrative makes sense is if the day the Jewish rulers went to the Romans was on the day after the preparation for the Sabbath but not yet on the Sabbath rest day itself. This could happen if this Sabbath preparation day was also the first day of the Feast of Unleavened Bread, because in that case, the Sabbath preparation would have been done two days before the Sabbath instead of the day before the Sabbath and the sequence would look like this: preparation for the Passover meal *and* the Sabbath feast were simultaneous to the Jewish leaders; the Passover meal happens and everyone is in their homes till morning; that morning would begin the normal Sabbath preparations, but because only cooking was allowed due to restrictions on the first day of the Feast of Unleavened Bread (we discuss this shortly), they had done all the preparation work the day before, the leaders are not under Sabbath "no walk" laws because it's not yet the beginning of the Sabbath rest; they walk to the rulers and ask for a guard to be placed—which conversation would not necessarily be considered work but information exchange which may explain why they posed the conversation suggesting that the Romans do the work (Mt 26:62-66); then the Sabbath sunset happens and Sabbath begins. All this considered, this timeframe appears to be m(x-4).

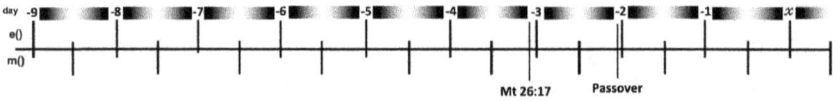

Mt 26:18   **"And he said, Go into the city to such a man, and say unto him, The Master saith, My time is at hand; I will keep the passover at thy house with my disciples."**

The question here revolves around the phrase "…I will keep the Passover at thy house…." Again, we see based on bias or conjecture the translation of the word "keep" because as translated, it sounds as if Jesus will eat the Passover with the disciples. However, the Greek word is poieo (ποιέω) which also means "to make ready; to prepare." It's used hundreds of times in Scripture as a primary infinitive for "to do" or "to make." The only way to interpret this is in context, and given the full context of Matthew's gospel, this could not be saying that Jesus would keep the Passover, but that Jesus would prepare for the Passover at the man's house. That makes this timeframe m(x-4).

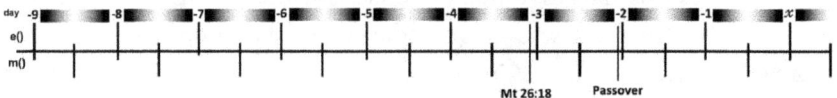

Lk 22:7-8   **"Then came the day of unleavened bread, when the passover must be killed. 8 And he sent Peter and John, saying, Go and prepare us the passover, that we may eat."**

The day of unleavened bread is at hand and Jesus sends Peter and John to prepare the meal. Note the entries for Mt 26:17 and Mt 26:18 for dialog on this. This is m(x-4).

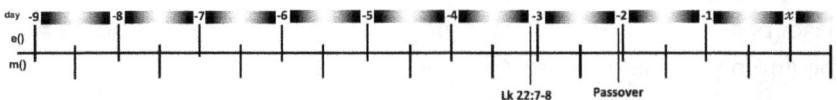

And finally, God bless John. His account is the one that helps us put all the other pieces together. Note the sequence that John states in Jn 13:1-4 and that he doesn't begin with the preparation like the other Gospel writers.

Jn 13:1-4   **"Now before the feast of the passover, when Jesus knew that his hour was come that he should depart out of this world unto the Father, having loved..."**
Continuing...

> his own which were in the world, he loved them unto the end. [2] And supper being ended [the one the disciples had just prepared], the devil having now put into the heart of Judas Iscariot, Simon's [son], to betray him; [3] Jesus knowing that the Father had given all things into his hands, and that he was come from God, and went to God; [4] He riseth from supper, and laid aside his garments; and took a towel, and girded himself."

John identifies the meal Jesus just completed with the disciples here in Jn 13:1-4 as something other than the Passover meal by use of the phrases "Now before the feast of passover...supper being ended...He riseth from supper." Passover begins toward nightfall on Nisan 14 and continues through Nisan15 as supper—the first meal of the day. This means the actions in Jn 13:1-4 happened on the evening of Nisan 14 and before the subsequent afternoon hours of Nisan 14 when the Passover sacrifice would be made. The preparation for this meal must have happened before sunset on Nisan 13 and this meal as the first meal of the day on Nisan 14, the day before the Feast of Unleavened Bread. Read here:

> Now before the feast of the passover, when Jesus knew that his hour was come that he should depart out of this world unto the Father... And supper being ended, the devil having now put into the heart of Judas Iscariot, Simon's [son], to betray him...He

riseth from supper, and laid aside his garments; and took a towel, and girded himself.

John identifies that this meal is before evening of Nisan 15 and that Judas has already determined to betray him, which happened on Nisan 13 after Jesus ate dinner at the house of Simon the Leper. That positions this Scripture in the following matrix:

- Judas already has in his heart to betray Jesus, which happened on m(x-5) or possibly, by that point, e(x-4);
- after the disciples prepare the meal on m(x-4);
- supper now being ended sometime in e(x-3), which was supper the evening after the disciples' preparation that just happened on m(x-4); and,
- before the feast of Passover that happens at sunset on m(x-3).

This narrative must begin before sunset on m(x-4) and then steps into supper on e(x-3). This Scripture happens in e(x-3).

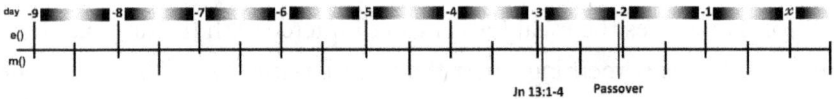

Jn 13:27-29   **"And after the sop Satan entered into him. Then said Jesus unto him, That thou doest, do quickly. [28] Now no man at the table knew for what intent he spake this unto him. [29] For some [of them] thought, because Judas had the bag, that Jesus had said unto him, Buy [those things] that we have need of against the feast; or, that he should give something to the poor."**

Jesus dismisses Judas at the end of the meal. The disciple's thoughts are recorded in this verse:

> [29] For some [of them] thought, because Judas had the bag, that Jesus had said unto him, Buy [those things] that we have need of against the feast; or, that he should give something to the poor.

Here are some logical fallacies to consider if one interprets the meal Jesus was eating as the Passover feast on Nisan 15. Why would Judas be sent to get the items for the feast if they had just finished the preparations and the feast itself? Further, if it was the feast night, people were to stay in their homes until morning, so Jesus would be encouraging Judas to break the Passover law by leaving to go shopping. Notable is that it's not yet morning, so this could not be the conclusion of the first day of the celebration of the Feast of Unleavened Bread that happens on the evening of Nisan 15, notwithstanding, John notes these events happening just before the feast, which begins in the hours just before sundown at the end of the 14th. That shows this Scripture happens on e(x-3).

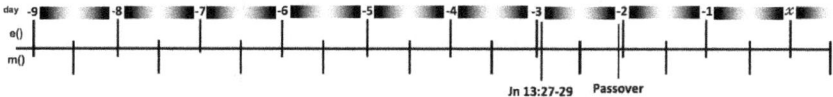

Mt 26:36   **"Then cometh Jesus with them unto a place called Gethsemane, and saith unto the disciples, Sit ye here, while I go and pray yonder."**

It seems unbelievable that Jesus would have cut short the first day of the Feast of Unleavened Bread and the in-leading Passover sacrifice and meat eating, given He was to celebrate that evening together with His co-celebrants, that the event was to take all night and that they were not to leave until morning. Consider Moses' instructions about celebrating Passover when, in Deuteronomy, he states:

> ...thou shalt sacrifice the Passover at even, at the going down of the sun, at the season that thou camest forth out of Egypt. And thou shalt roast and eat it in the place which the LORD thy God shall choose: and though shalt turn in the morning, and go unto thy tents (Deut. 16: 6b-7).

Also, Exodus 12:21-27 states:

²¹ Then Moses called for all the elders of Israel, and said unto them, Draw out and take you a lamb according to your families, and kill the passover. ²² And ye shall take a bunch of hyssop, and dip [it] in the blood that [is] in the bason, and strike the lintel and the two side posts with the blood that [is] in the bason; and none of you shall go out at the door of his house until the morning. ²³ For the LORD will pass through to smite the Egyptians; and when he seeth the blood upon the lintel, and on the two side posts, the LORD will pass over the door, and will not suffer the destroyer to come in unto your houses to smite [you]. ²⁴ And ye shall observe this thing for an ordinance to thee and to thy sons for ever. ²⁵ And it shall come to pass, when ye be come to the land which the LORD will give you, according as he hath promised, that ye shall keep this service. ²⁶ And it shall come to pass, when your children shall say unto you, What mean ye by this service? ²⁷ That ye shall say, It [is] the sacrifice of the LORD'S passover, who passed over the houses of the children of Israel in Egypt, when he smote the Egyptians, and delivered our houses. And the people bowed the head and worshipped.

The Nisan 14 evening started an event that was to last well into the next morning and that was to be celebrated with staff in hand and ready to go (Ex 12:8-11). Even assuming Jesus and the disciples were able to eat all the lamb that was roasted as Deut. 16:4 demands, preparing for a minimum of 13 people (as Judas and Jesus were expected to be there) would have required more than one lamb and to roast both of them from a raw state and then consume the entirety of the lambs before leaving for the garden of Gethsemane is unlikely.

Also, the preparation that Peter and John completed would not have included the lamb because it could not be roasted until sunset according to the feast mandate because the Passover lamb must be sacrificed by the priest at the place appointed by God and returned to the family to take home and roast. They would only have prepared the setting, cleaned the dwelling of all leaven (yeast, representing sin), and prepared the rest of the meal's elements. They would then have waited for the lambs to be killed and bled so that the lamb could be placed on a spit to roast over a fire (Ex 12:8-11).

Also, we have reference in multiple gospels that the Jews did not want to make an uproar on the feast days, underscoring that this day when Jesus ate with the disciples and then went to Gethsemane where He was ultimately arrested could not have been toward nightfall hours of Nisan 14 or even after sunset beginning the day of Nisan 15. This verse would have occurred on the evening prior to m(x-3) making this event happen on e(x-3).

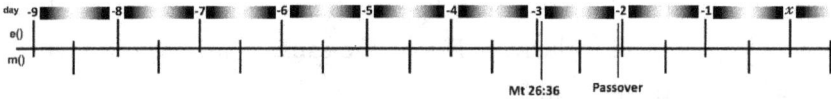

Before continuing forward, you must understand the difference between doing "no work" on the Sabbath feast and doing "no servile work" on the first and last days of the Feast of Unleavened Bread. The priests, indeed the whole nation of Israel, were bound by the law to do no work at all on Sabbath feast days and to do no *servile* work on the first and last feast days of the Feast of Unleavened Bread. Please understand the difference between these two before studying further as your understanding these two terms ("no work" and "no servile work") will be pivotal.

Servile Work   **The definition of "servile work" is very important as no servile work was allowed on the first and last days of the Feast of Unleavened Bread. It is different from the "no work" mandate of the weekly Sabbath feast.**

This is not the same as "no work" allowed on the weekly Sabbath feast. While the word in Hebrew for "work" is the same, the modifier for "servile" invokes a separate meaning to the restriction.

On the Sabbath, the people were not even allowed to kindle a fire (Ex. 35:3) and were told to stay in their homes but, the restriction for "no servile work" on the first day of the Feast of Unleavened Bread is different. Searching Scripture for the understanding of servile work leads one to Exodus 12:16 that specifically discusses the work allowed on the first and last days of the Feast of Unleavened Bread and that reads:

> And in the first day there shall be an holy
> convocation, and in the seventh day there shall be an
> holy convocation to you; no manner of work shall be
> done in them, save that which every man must eat,
> that only may be done of you. (Exodus 12:16)

The word for "work" (מְלָאכָה – měla'kah) means one's occupation; service; public, political or religious business; making or doing something: it is all inclusive. This is the same word used in Genesis 2:2 where God ended all His work.

In this verse from Exodus 12, we see that no work is allowed on the first and last days of the celebration except what is identified by the modifying phrase, "...save that which every man must eat, that only may be done of you." This signifies the normal Sabbath is different from the first feast day, but the word "servile" is not used in this verse.

However, Leviticus 23:6-8 gives us the reference to link "servile work" with the definition we just read of "no manner of work...save that which every man must eat" as we read:

> And on the fifteenth day of the same month is the
> feast of unleavened bread unto the LORD: seven
> days ye must eat unleavened bread. In the first day ye
> shall have an holy convocation: ye shall do no servile
> work therein. But ye shall offer an offering made by
> fire unto the LORD seven days: in the seventh
> day is an holy convocation: ye shall do no servile
> work therein.

The words "servile work" are a subset of duties (מְלָאכָה – měla'kah). The word "servile" is (עֲבֹדָה – `abodah) any labor that is to the service and benefit of others – including service in the work of God's temple duties (i.e. temple service, sacrifice, and maintaining His house).

Servile work does not appear to encompass Sabbath distances for walking, types of conversations or interactions, only labors that didn't include cooking food.

Notable is that Lev 23:24-25 notes that another Jewish feast, the feast of Trumpets, begins the 7th month and first day, with no servile work; however, on the day of Atonement, which is the 7th month and 10th day, they shall do no work at all on that feast day. Lev. 23:32 states:

> It shall be unto you a sabbath of rest, and ye shall afflict your souls: in the ninth day of the month at even, from even unto even, shall ye celebrate your sabbath.

So, there are definite differences between servile work and Sabbath rest. This is upheld in Lev 23:3 when the Lord explains the weekly Sabbath feast. This is notable because for Passover, no servile work is permitted, but it is not the absolute restriction to Sabbath feast rules.

Please note that the first and last days of the Feast of Unleavened Bread are *not* called sabbaths in the Scripture, despite current changes in interpretation, culture or practice and are not treated as sabbath days in Scripture interactions.

Understanding this is important, because the priests, scribes, temple guard, Sanhedrin and other Jewish authorities could not arrest Jesus, try Jesus, crucify Jesus or meet on a Sabbath day for temple business. Further, they could not do these things on the first or last day of the Feast of Unleavened Bread, or they would be breaking the law. As we read further into the crucifixion account, keep this in mind: Jewish leaders cannot transact the duties of their religious or political service on the Sabbath feast, or the first and last days of the Feast of Unleavened Bread.

Lk 22:52   **"Then Jesus said unto the chief priests, and captains of the temple, and the elders, which were come to him, Be ye come out, as against a thief, with swords and staves?"**

It seems highly unlikely that the chief priests, captains of the temple and elders would all break Passover law and leave their families during their Passover feast celebration to come to Gethsemane and deal with Jesus. If the meal that Jesus ate was the Passover feast, that would make the current time the evening of Nisan 15 (which happens before morning Nisan 15), which is the first day of the Feast of Unleavened Bread where "no servile work" can be done by any of the nation of Israel meaning they would have had to break the law to bring Jesus before Caiaphas or for the Sanhedrin to meet. Further, they would have left their homes, against the command of God to Moses as explained in the entry for Mt 26:36 (i.e. Deut 16:6b-7; Ex 12:8-27). This is e(x-3).

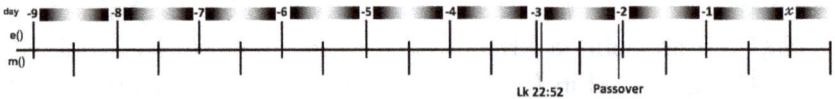

Mk 14:43-15:47 "And immediately, while he yet spake, cometh Judas, one of the twelve, and with him a great multitude with swords and staves, from the chief priests and the scribes and the elders."

This section of Scripture begins at Mk 14:43 and goes all the way to Mk 15:47 where we end with, "And Mary Magdalene and Mary [the mother] of Joses beheld where he was laid."

Starting at Mk 14:43 and going through Mk 15:47 we observe the chronological history of the betrayal through the entombment of Jesus, and it is highly unlikely that Jesus would have eaten the Passover meal and that the events surrounding Jesus' life would have happened on the first day of the feast or a Sabbath feast, because these actions would not be allowed for the Jews. So, these had to happen before the Sabbath and before the Passover sacrifice the end of the day on Nisan 14, making this time frame e(x-3) to m(x-3) and Judas coming to the garden of Gethsemane at e(x-3).

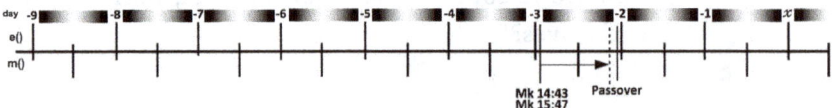

Jn 18:28-29	**"Then led they Jesus from Caiaphas unto the hall of judgment: and it was early; and they themselves went not into the judgment hall, lest they should be defiled; but that they might eat the passover. ²⁹ Pilate then went out unto them, and said, What accusation bring ye against this man?"**

The men, officers and Pharisees (Jn 18:3) [possibly the priests per Jn 18:35] would not go into the hall of judgment "...lest they should be defiled; but that they might eat the Passover." Does this mean they didn't want to be defiled to eat some sub-portion of the seven-day Passover feast (suggesting this event is happening a day or two into the feast and lasts less than the feast); does it mean the remainder of the feast (that if they went into the judgment hall they could not finish the feast); does it mean the Passover meal itself on Nisan 15; or, does it mean the Passover lamb—since the Greek word "Pascha," which is translated "Passover," can represent all three items: the feast, the actual meal on Nisan 15 and the Passover lamb itself sacrificed at sundown on Nisan 14. From what were they protecting their cleanness?

Leviticus 22:1-7 discusses the uncleanness that would likely be encountered by a priest going into the Roman dwelling, where vv. 5-7 specifically deal with restrictions on the sons of Aaron from touching anything another unclean man has touched. The uncleanness was remediated by water and lasted until evening after sunset:

> ⁵ Or whosoever touches any creeping thing, whereby he may be made unclean, or a man of whom he may take uncleanness, whatsoever uncleanness he hath; ⁶ the soul which touched any such shall be unclean until even, and shall not eat of the holy things, unless he wash his flesh with water. ⁷ And when the sun is down, he shall be clean, and shall afterward eat of the holy things; because it is his food.

The Holy Things were the temple portions going to the priests.

In Lev 22, we see that the priests could be made unclean if they even touched something another unclean man had touched. It makes their reason not to enter Pilate's dwelling understandable.

In context, this applied to the priesthood as verse two states,

> Speak to Aaron and to his sons, that they separate themselves from the holy things of the children of Israel, and that they profane not my holy name in those things which they hallow unto me: I am the LORD.

We know it was the priests and officers who were vying for Jesus' crucifixion because John captures this fact in Jn 18:25 and 19:6

> [25] Pilate answered, Am I a Jew? Thine own nation and the chief priests have delivered thee unto me: what hast thou done? ... [6] When the chief priests therefore and officers saw him, they cried out, saying, Crucify [him], crucify [him]. Pilate saith unto them, Take ye him, and crucify [him]: for I find no fault in him.

It was possible for the cleansed priests to sacrifice the Passover offering for others if those who were bringing the Passover sacrifice were unclean, but if priests their selves were unclean, they could not sacrifice for their selves or others. The priest sacrificing the Passover offering for someone who was unclean was not the norm, as everyone was expected to cleanse their self before the sacrifice, which was why people were coming to Jerusalem at least a week before the Passover (Jn 11:55-Jn 12:1), to fulfill Passover cleansing rituals. However, in the following old testament example, we see where an exception was made; but the priests had to be cleansed, even to offer for these unclean:

> [15] Then they killed the passover on the fourteenth [day] of the second month: and the priests and the Levites were ashamed, and sanctified themselves, and brought in the burnt offerings into the house of

the LORD. [16] And they stood in their place after their manner, according to the law of Moses the man of God: the priests sprinkled the blood, [which they received] of the hand of the Levites. [17] For [there were] many in the congregation that were not sanctified: therefore the Levites had the charge of the killing of the passovers for every one [that was] not clean, to sanctify [them] unto the LORD. [18] For a multitude of the people, [even] many of Ephraim, and Manasseh, Issachar, and Zebulun, had not cleansed themselves, yet did they eat the passover otherwise than it was written. But Hezekiah prayed for them, saying, The good LORD pardon every one [19] [That] prepareth his heart to seek God, the LORD God of his fathers, though [he be] not [cleansed] according to the purification of the sanctuary. [20] And the LORD hearkened to Hezekiah, and healed the people. — 2Ch 30:15-18

The conclusion? This priestly uncleanness, by entering the Roman judgment hall, would not affect the entire Passover celebration of the priests or even numerous days of their celebration since there would be time for any priest to wash, wait for the sun to set, and then to eat the evening dinner. The uncleanness feared in this verse can only apply to the offering of the Passover sacrifice itself. One must be clean to make the offering in the evening before sunset: the sacrifice itself could not be made if the priest was unclean, because the offering would happen before the person was made clean at sunset. If the priests were defiled, they could not touch the Passover sacrifice on behalf of the families of Israel; they could not sacrifice their own Passover sacrifice for their own Passover meal. Transgressing this law results in the following verse 9 of Leviticus 22:

> They shall therefore keep mine ordinance, lest they
> bear sin for it, and die therefore, if they profane it: I
> the LORD do sanctify them.

Just because God had extended grace in one specific unordinary instance with Hezekiah did not mean the priests would try it a second time to test the Lord.

Being clean of moral and spiritual filth was a requirement for the Passover feast, for priest and individual alike. We've discussed the burden carried by the priests, but the individual carried responsibility too. Rules on cleanness and uncleanness that affected all those who were celebrating and making the offering who were not priests are visible in the following Scriptures:

- [2Ch 35:6] So kill the passover, and sanctify yourselves, and prepare your brethren, that [they] may do according to the word of the LORD by the hand of Moses. [There were sanctification requirements to celebrate.]

- [Num 9:13] But the man that [is] clean, and is not in a journey, and forbeareth to keep the passover, even the same soul shall be cut off from among his people: because he brought not the offering of the LORD in his appointed season, that man shall bear his sin. [Cleanness was expected and upon being clean the celebration expected to be kept.]

- [2Ch 30:18] For a multitude of the people, [even] many of Ephraim, and Manasseh, Issachar, and Zebulun, had not cleansed themselves, yet did they eat the passover otherwise than it was written. [God expects self-preparation and cleanliness before the Passover may be celebrated.]

- [Num 9:6-7, 10-11] [6] And there were certain men, who were defiled by the dead body of a man, that they could not keep the passover on that day: and they came before Moses and before Aaron on that day: [7] And those men said unto him, We [are] defiled by the dead body of a man: wherefore are we kept back, that we may not offer an offering of the LORD in his appointed season among the children of Israel? ... [10] Speak unto the children of Israel, saying, If any man of you or of your posterity shall be unclean by reason of a dead body, or [be] in a journey afar off, yet he shall keep the passover unto the LORD. [11] The fourteenth day of the second month at even they shall keep it, [and] eat it with unleavened bread and bitter [herbs].

So then, the priests and leaders understood that they could become unclean and unable to celebrate the Passover and to perform their duties, and these individuals were evidently afraid (whether justifiably or not) that entering the judgment hall would make them unclean and unable to celebrate or perform their Passover responsibilities as the sun was setting that same day, which is the commandment:

> ...thou shalt sacrifice the Passover at even, at the
> going down of the sun, at the season that thou
> camest forth out of Egypt. And thou shalt roast and
> eat it in the place which the LORD thy God shall
> choose: and thou shalt turn in the morning, and go
> unto thy tents (Deut. 16: 6b-7).

The conclusion, then, is that the time of this Scripture must relate directly to the period just before sunset at the end of Nisan 14 and to the sacrifice of the Passover lamb itself. The priests could wash, but the uncleanness would last until the second after the sun sets, which is not a problem for any day except Nisan 14 since the Passover lambs need to be sacrificed at evening, at the going down of the sun, and the priesthood must be finished with the nation's sacrifices before dark on Nisan 14, which would begin the Feast of Unleavened Bread on Nisan 15.

The same would hold true with the man offering the lamb of Passover for his family: he could not do so if he were unclean. So while they could eat the Feast of Unleavened Bread if it were already prepared (they could wash and by supper be clean again), because the sacrifice and the beginning of the celebration happens before sunset, they cannot touch the lamb while unclean, and thus cannot sacrifice it, offer it, or cook it and would be ineligible for the first day of the feast, something God didn't allow unless: 1) they had touched a dead body, or 2) were out of town (2 Chron 30:2). That places this Scripture about leading Jesus to see Caiaphas and then to the judgment hall on e(x-3) or early m(x-3).

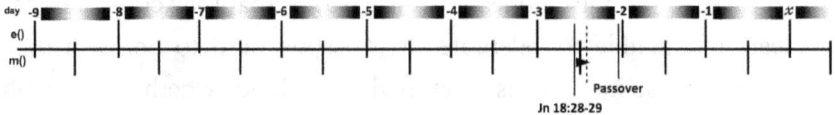

Jn 18:28-29

Mk 15:1   **"And straightway in the morning the chief priests held a consultation with the elders and scribes and the whole council, and bound Jesus, and carried *him* away, and delivered *him* to Pilate."**

It was the chief priests, elders, scribes and whole council who consorted against Jesus to deliver Him to Pilate according to gospel writer Mark. Mark records this happening the immediate morning after Jesus' supper with the disciples and the garden of Gethsemane making this m(after gethsemane), which would be m(x-3).

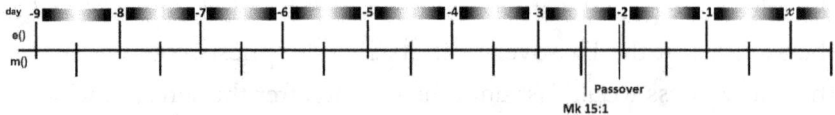

Mk 15:1

Lk 22:66-23:1   **"And as soon as it was day, the elders of the people and the chief priests and the scribes came together, and led him into their council...[1] And the whole multitude of them arose, and led him unto Pilate."**

It was the elders, chief priests and scribes who arose and went to Pilate. Luke records it was the morning after the dinner with the disciples that was followed by the garden of gethsemane making this m(after Gethsemane), which would be m(x-3).

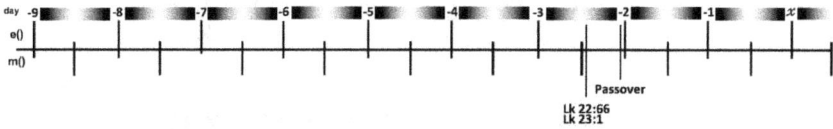

Jesus' interaction with Pilate offers a few hints on the chronology of the entire happening. Consider what Luke and John both reference as they incorporate the Roman view of the Passover celebration with the trial of Jesus.

Lk 23:16-17   **"I will therefore chastise him, and release [him].** [17] **(For of necessity he must release one unto them at the feast.)" – Pilate**

This is covered in more detail in the next entries on Jn 18:39 and 19:5-18a. Here, though, remembering the previous observations of the priests, Pilate's prisoner release would be in honor of the feast at the beginning and before an uproar could occur. This must be m(x-3).

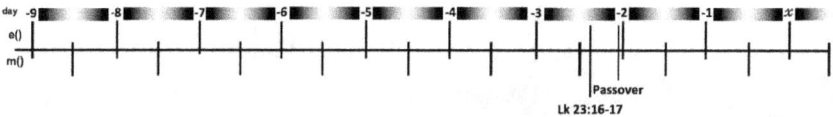

Jn 18:39   **"But ye have a custom, that I should release unto you one at the passover: will ye therefore that I release unto you the King of the Jews?" – Pilate**

Pilate identifies that he releases a prisoner to the Jews "at the Passover." Mt 27:15, Mk 15:6, Lk 23:17 all state this was done at the Passover. Given that the Jewish leaders did not want to make an uproar by this happening on a feast day, it only stands to reason this must be before the actual Nisan 14 sacrifice and Nisan 15 feast making this m(x-3).

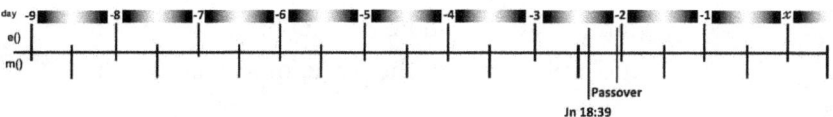

Jn 19:5-18a **"Then came Jesus forth, wearing the crown of thorns, and the purple robe. And [Pilate] saith unto them, Behold the man! 6 When the chief priests therefore and officers saw him, they cried out, saying, Crucify [him], crucify [him]. Pilate saith unto them, Take ye him, and crucify [him]: for I find no fault in him."**

John 18:39 is further underscored by John's continued text in Jn 19:5-6, 12-18a [emphasis added] which reads:

> 5 Then came Jesus forth, wearing the crown of thorns, and the purple robe. And [Pilate] saith unto them, Behold the man! 6 When the **chief priests therefore and officers saw him**, they cried out, saying, Crucify [him], crucify [him]. Pilate saith unto them, Take ye him, and crucify [him]: for I find no fault in him. ... 12 And from thenceforth Pilate sought to release him: but the Jews cried out, saying, If thou let this man go, thou art not Caesar's friend: whosoever maketh himself a king speaketh against Caesar. 13 When Pilate therefore heard that saying, he brought Jesus forth, and sat down in the judgment seat in a place that is called the Pavement, but in the Hebrew, Gabbatha. 14 **And it was the preparation of the passover, and about the sixth hour**: and he saith unto the Jews, Behold your King! 15 But they cried out, Away with [him], away with [him], crucify him. Pilate saith unto them, Shall I crucify your King? The chief priests answered, We have no king but Caesar. 16 Then delivered he him therefore unto them to be crucified. And they took Jesus, and led [him] away. 17 And he bearing his cross went forth into a place called [the place] of a skull, which is

called in the Hebrew Golgotha: [18] Where they crucified him....

The point here is that Pilate wanted to release Jesus because "at the Passover" there was a customary release of a prisoner. John notes this happens on the day people are preparing for their Passover meal. This Scripture standing alone doesn't say the exact date, but it does tell us the relative position because we know the disciples had already prepared for their Passover feast, so the meal had to be close and v. 14 states it is the preparation for the Passover, this time for the rest of the nation of Israel, and *this* preparation for Israel is happening while Jesus' trial is unfolding and He is now being crucified.

We also know that the custom was to release one at the feast, which started on Nisan 14 in the evening with the feast proper beginning sunset on Nisan 15; we know the Jewish leaders didn't want Jesus handed over on Nisan 15 and possibly Nisan 15-Nisan 21; we know that two days prior to the Passover He was at Simon the Leper's house. It leaves only one day: Jesus was at Simon the Lepers house two days before; the next day He was with the disciples eating supper; that night He was in the garden and the next morning, Jesus is here in front of Pilate, and this day is the preparation for the Passover as celebrated by those who were not disciples with Jesus, and the Sabbath followed. This therefore must be m(x-3).

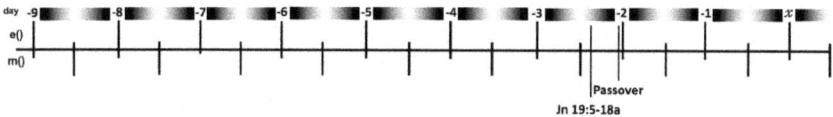

Passover
Jn 19:5-18a

Chapter End Notes/Observations

THE POST-SACRIFICIAL EVENTS

N ow we enter Jesus' post-sacrificial Scriptures. The time from Pilate to Jesus' death has just transpired. The scriptures all dealing with the actual crucifixion events their selves happen on the same day. We know this because we have record of the number of hours transpiring during the event. So, here, we continue: Jesus is dead and still on the cross as we enter the following verses.

Mk 15:42   **"And now when the even was come, because it was the preparation, that is, the day before the sabbath...."**

The focus here is on the word "preparation" and the phrase "the day before the sabbath." Leading into the crucifixion, it was the preparation for the Passover; now, we have to examine if the focus changes to the preparation for the Sabbath. "And now when even was come...." Even[ing] falls after the ninth hour all the way to sunset. Stating it was "the preparation" means it was the preparation for a feast, whether a Sabbath feast or the Feast of Unleavened Bread is inconclusive since the same word is used for both; we just know it was before the Sabbath; we don't know which feast was the focus of the preparation. The Sabbath feast and the Feast of Unleavened Bread are both considered feasts of the Lord (cf. Lev 23:3 for Sabbath and Lev 23:5-6 for Passover and the Feast of Unleavened Bread). So, the word "preparation" itself is not definitive. Then the phrase "the day before the sabbath" is the Greek word (προσάββατον – prosabbaton) which only means "before sabbath" and carries no ordinal position. This word is only used once here in the New Testament and twice in the Septuagint (the Greek copy of the old testament as a translation from Hebrew). The other places we find this word are outside of Scripture which is another way we come to understand meaning of vocabulary, for example, this term was used in the book of Judith.

In all cases, the word (προσάββατον – prosabbaton) is identified as the day preceding the Sabbath by nature of the context of the writing not by grammatical formulation. This is very important. We have no example of the word (προσάββατον – prosabbaton) being used differently than "the preparation the day before the sabbath"; however, given its very scant use, that hardly suggests that the word "day" is always mandatory in the translation. The word "pros" means "before" and "sabbaton" means "sabbath." The "before-sabbath" preparation maintains its definition even with a wider span of days between the preparation and the Sabbath day, so if there were one day, two days or three days between the preparation and the Sabbath day itself, the word "prosabbaton" would still be correct: a translation or understanding is not jeopardized in any of these circumstances.

To state that the word "day" should always be included in the translation would only hold value if there were other ample examples in Scripture or other Greek literature where there were multiple days between the preparation and the Sabbath and the word (προσάββατον – prosabbaton) was *still* used to represent the singular and specific day before the Sabbath, even in those cases. In absence of such language in multiple sources to show standardized use, it is conjecture to assume the preparation is always the day before the Sabbath as the word only states "before sabbath" with no ordinal position enforced in its structure.

Therefore, without jeopardizing the translation in Mk 15:42, it could as specifically read:

> And now when the eve was come [after the 9th hour
> and before sunset] because it was the preparation,
> that is, before sabbath, Joseph of Arimathea, an
> honorable counselor, which also waited for the
> kingdom of God, came and went in boldly unto
> Pilate, and craved the body of Jesus.

If the day following Jesus' crucifixion was a day where work was not allowed, which is true regarding the first day of the Feast of Unleavened Bread (Lev. 23:7) where only food preparation is permissible, then the use of (προσάββατον – prosabbaton) is accurate to its construction (pros-sabbaton = before sabbath) and still accurate in all other uses as well since the context of the verses determines the interpretation. In other words, there could have been a preparation that was for the Feast of Unleavened Bread as well as the Sabbath feast on the day that Jesus was crucified. The context of this verse makes this day m(x-3).

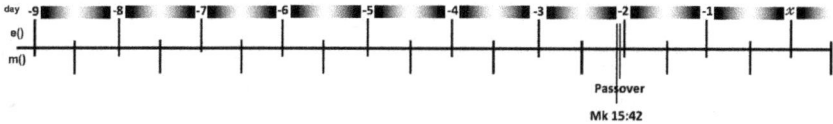

Jn 19:31   **"The Jews therefore, because it was the preparation, that the bodies should not remain upon the cross on the sabbath day,"**

Continuing…

> (for that sabbath day was an high day,) besought
> Pilate that their legs might be broken, and [that] they
> might be taken away."

The Sabbath after the preparation is identified by the phrase, "for that sabbath day was a high day." The intent is that they wanted the crucified down before evening began, because that Sabbath which was coming was a high day. This verse gives no sense of the time as to when the Sabbath would commence, only that they wanted the bodies down before it did. This could have been up to four days away from a physiological view, since crucifixion would often take days, as the people would die a slow death. If the day following the crucifixion was the first day of the Feast of Unleavened Bread, when no servile work could occur, this Scripture would still be true. The bodies could not be interred on the first feast day without possibly defiling those caring for the dead and without the caretakers facing work limitations. The same would be true during the Sabbath feast.

Deuteronomy 21:22-23 deals with another main reason they wanted the bodies down: because it would affect the sanctity of the nation during the celebration as well:

> If a man has committed a sin deserving of death, and he is put to death, and you hang him on a tree, [23] his body shall not remain overnight on the tree, but you shall surely bury him that day, so that you do not defile the land which the Lord your God is giving you as an inheritance; for he who is hanged is accursed of God.

Next, that any given Sabbath or celebration is a "high day" is never defined in Scripture even though current tradition suggests an interpretation. It may be considered a "high day" Sabbath because it occurs simultaneously on the first day of the Feast of Unleavened Bread—but, this is not defined by Scripture; it would only be an assumption. What we do know is that something in the life of John, the gospel writer, caused him to see this day as great, special and of a grand scale (gk. μέγας – megas) and different than other Sabbath days, "for **that** sabbath day was an high day."

The take-away, then, is that it was a preparation day; the Sabbath was coming; and without intervention, the bodies could have been there on the Sabbath; that Sabbath was a high day—signifying something special or different in the recognition of author John. Since we don't have a number of days before or between "preparation" and "sabbath" and since the Jews didn't want to leave the bodies hanging on a feast day, we have to assume this preparation was during the morning period [sunrise to sunset] of Nisan 14 and the Sabbath was sometime after this. A Friday crucifixion would make the historical events that follow quite improbable if not impossible because the Jewish leaders would not work on the Sabbath day and would be forced to repetitively break the laws of Moses to carry it out. This chronology seems to be unfolding such that this event must occur on m(x-3) and where the next day is not yet the Sabbath feast.

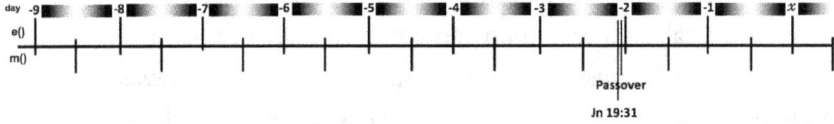

Passover

Jn 19:31

Lk 23:54,56	"And that day was the preparation, and the sabbath drew on. ... 56 And they returned, and prepared spices and ointments; and rested the sabbath day according to the commandment."

These Scriptures reference the day Jesus was crucified and placed in the tomb. So, in the lives of Jesus and the disciples (we have no way of knowing if anyone else did or not) Peter and John prepared the meal that Jesus ate on the day before the crucifixion (Lk 22:7-13); then there was another preparation on the day of the crucifixion for the nation of Israel (Lk 23:54)… "and the sabbath drew on" (v. 54). If this second "preparation" was the preparation of the Feast of Unleavened Bread (or perhaps both the Feast of Unleavened Bread and the ensuing Sabbath feast) with the Sabbath following the next evening, the translation and chronology would still be correct and not jeopardized.

Why did Luke use the word "drew on" (ἐπιφώσκω—epiphōskō)? It is only used twice in Scripture and both times it refrences the period between Jesus' death and resurrection. It seems that "drew on" in Luke means what it does in Mt 28:1—that it was "dawning" and not that it had arrived or was as close as stating, "and the Sabbath was the next day." This is also supported by the imperfect tense, active voice, indicative mood of the verb "drew on" meaning it was a continuing, repetitive and yet unterminated action—the Sabbath was out of reach; it kept coming but had not yet arrived, suggesting to us that we should keep reading to find when it finally does arrive. The account would then be modified by verse 56 and end in Lk 24:1.

So, all we have is the following chronology: there was a preparation (for Passover feast and/or Sabbath feast, we don't know as the same word is used for both); the Sabbath was beyond touch; there was enough time to do a small amount of physical labor before sunset; there was a sabbath rest; then came the first day of the week. There is nothing in the language that commands the preparation was a sabbath preparation done specifically on the day before the Sabbath, only that it happened for Sabbath. This would be a correct translation even if the next day was the first day of the Feast of Unleavened Bread and the Sabbath feast the day after that, because on that first Unleavened Bread feast day, they could "do no servile work" and would not have been able to prepare anything other than food to eat—no tomb preparations. So if m(x-3) was preparation for Passover, the next day e(x-2) was the normal Sabbath preparation, it would also be Nisan 15 and they would have needed to do two days of food preparation at once (both Passover meal and Sabbath meal), but no other work, in order to honor God's feast celebration laws. This Scripture happens at m(x-3).

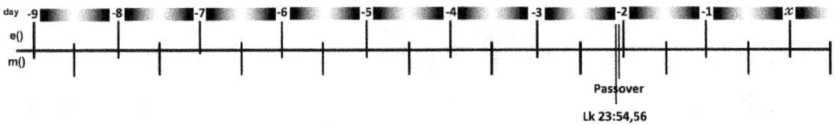

As we move more into Jesus' post-sacrifice events, consider the burial of Jesus and the interactions by Joseph of Arimathea and Nicodemus. No doubt, they wanted to celebrate the Passover with their families, because this feast was a very important and special part of the Jewish calendar and the first feast of the calendar year. They had to consider the cost of taking care of Jesus' body because doing so most likely caused them to forfeit celebrating the feast with everyone else. What happens when a Jew touches a dead body before the

Passover meal and the successive days of the Feast of Unleavened Bread? Consider the following Scriptures:

Num 9:6-13   **"And there were certain men, who were defiled by the dead body of a man, that they could not keep the passover on that day: and they came before Moses and before Aaron on that day...."**

Here is the rest of that section of Scripture. Read carefully the importance of the Passover feast.

> [7] And those men said unto him, We [are] defiled by the dead body of a man: wherefore are we kept back, that we may not offer an offering of the LORD in his appointed season among the children of Israel? [8] And Moses said unto them, Stand still, and I will hear what the LORD will command concerning you. [9] And the LORD spake unto Moses, saying, [10] Speak unto the children of Israel, saying, If any man of you or of your posterity shall be unclean by reason of a dead body, or [be] in a journey afar off, yet he shall keep the passover unto the LORD. [11] The fourteenth day of the second month at even they shall keep it, [and] eat it with unleavened bread and bitter [herbs]. [12] They shall leave none of it unto the morning, nor break any bone of it: according to all the ordinances of the passover they shall keep it. [13] But the man that [is] clean, and is not in a journey, and forbeareth to keep the passover, even the same soul shall be cut off from among his people: because he brought not the offering of the LORD in his appointed season, that man shall bear his sin.

This feast was very important to God and to the people, so much so, that God made two allowances so that people could honor it and not be cut off from the nation of Israel, one of which was caring for the dead. Touching a dead body would force the feast celebrant to wait a month before being able to celebrate. If this were you, it would likely feel similar to celebrating your birthday by yourself because this was a national celebration with a lot of interaction.

Num 19:11-22 **"He that toucheth the dead body of any man shall be unclean seven days..."**

Please read Numbers 19:11-22 in your Bible and then return here to continue. Whoever is unclean because of touching a dead body must wait a month and celebrate Passover on the second month and the 14th day at sunset, and not with the rest of the nation. It would also put you in a series of purification requirements that would last a week in order to be restored to a place of worship. This would be a large sacrifice for the men taking care of Jesus.

Unclean	**The state of being spiritually impure resulting in one's inability to enter God's presence for the purpose of worship or the fulfillment of some service that requires purity. The closer one came to God's presence in worship and service, the more purity was required; therefore, more stringent purity requirements exist for Jewish priests than for the average person.**

What we've discussed here is the topic of becoming "unclean" for the purpose of worship. To that end, understand that the priests, the sons of Aaron would be unclean if they touch anything that was touched by an unclean person, which suggests that if a priest touches the cloth wrapping a dead body, he would be unclean, or if he steps into a dwelling that is unclean, he will be unclean. For the priests, becoming unclean, on this day specifically, meant they could not perform their priestly duties for offering the Passover sacrifice for the people of Israel or for their own homes. For the average person, it also appears according to Numbers 19:22 that anyone touching Jesus, even wrapped in a shroud, would be unclean. For Joseph of Arimathea and Nicodemus, it meant they chose to sacrifice the Passover celebration with their families, friends and the entire nation of Israel and to postpone their celebration until the next month when they would celebrate it alone or possibly together, but without their families.

Jn 19:40	**"Then took they the body of Jesus, and wound it in linen clothes with the spices, as the manner of the Jews is to bury."**

They "wound" Jesus' body in linen. Note it says "clothes" and not "cloths." This verse references so much with so few words[iv]. The Scripture doesn't tell us specifics about how they wound Jesus' body, and because I want to keep the study at this point to only Scripture, I will include a later section dealing in detail with extra-biblical findings.

Interesting here is that the Greek word has many meanings, among them is to wind or twist. It can mean to twist on the corners also. It is possible that Jesus' body was laid in the cloth and the ends twisted to be used as handles. Just as interesting as this observation is that there is no specific word in Greek for "shroud," the name of the burial cloth in which the dead are laid and a word that has been used in Judaism since the first century. Further intrigue revolves around the Hebrew word for Shroud (תכריך) which means "to wind" even though history shows that the Jews did not wind (as a mummy) their dead. So, I submit the term "wound...as the manner of the Jews is to bury" is intended to create a mental image in the mind of the reader to clarify the difference between the Jewish burial process and other people groups who bury their dead differently. Since the Jews are not recognized for winding their dead or wrapping their dead in strips or lengths of cloth, I suggest the possibility of John stating that Jesus was enshrouded and since no word for "shroud" exists in the Greek, the phrase "wound ("shroud" in Hebrew)...as the manner of the Jews..." was his way of using existing Greek to communicate the Hebrew phrase, "Jesus was enshrouded."

For a more in-depth, extra-biblical analysis of this phrase, read the later section titled, *Observations from the Mishnah.* Irrespective of any preparation specifics, taking Jesus' body to the tomb would be before sunset on the day of the Passover sacrifice, making this m(x-3).

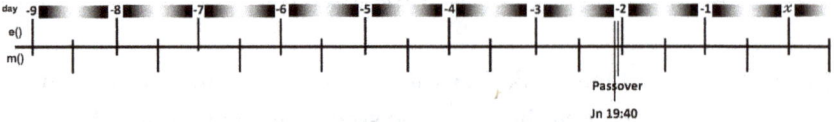

Mt 27:62-66   **"Now the next day, that followed the day of the preparation, the chief priests and Pharisees came together unto Pilate,"**

Here is the remainder of this section:

> [63] Saying, Sir, we remember that that deceiver said, while he was yet alive, After three days I will rise again. [64] Command therefore that the sepulchre be made sure until the third day, lest his disciples come by night, and steal him away, and say unto the people, He is risen from the dead: so the last error shall be worse than the first. [65] Pilate said unto them, Ye have a watch: go your way, make it as sure as ye can. [66] So they went, and made the sepulchre sure, sealing the stone, and setting a watch."

If this was the Sabbath, why wouldn't Matthew have said so? While I realize absence of language doesn't necessarily mean anything, we must remember that gospel writers used phrases like "…and the sabbath drew on…" to illustrate this time period. Why do the gospel writers have such difficulty calling this day what it is?

An evaluation of the phrase "Now the next day, that followed the preparation…" in verse 62 is valuable. If that was the typical Sabbath preparation from sunset Thursday to sunset Friday, it would make this Mt 27:62 verse happen on Saturday morning, which is a time where the priests and leaders would be bound by all Sabbath restrictions to do no work, including: restrictions for walking, laboring, political and temple services, as well as cooking and etcetera. Remember, for Sabbath feast, each person was told to stay in his place (Ex 16:29). However, if the day after Jesus' crucifixion was the first day of the feast on Nisan 15 and not yet the Sabbath, then Mt 27:62-66 would be permissible as all they did was have a conversation with the Romans and follow them as an entourage to the tomb where the Roman seal was affixed.[v] They did no servile work in honor of the Scripture, were not commanding their own servants or workers, and were not bound by the Sabbath rest restrictions since the first and last days of the "holy convocation" are not called "sabbath" days.

Interesting, too, is that it is called "the day following the day of preparation" suggesting that the day being discussed had multiple definitions or none at all, otherwise why not use the name of the day, like "the sabbath"? I suggest the writer understood that the day after the day of preparation was: before the Sabbath and also the first day of the Feast of Unleavened Bread and so he kept the term generic since two definitions for the same day existed and choosing one would run the risk of excluding the unused term or prioritizing the one chosen.

Also noteworthy is that in this account, we have no reference to the priests and pharisees standing outside the Roman dwelling. The absence of the information doesn't mean it didn't happen...but it did spark an interesting thought. On the day of the Passover preparation, one gospel states that the rulers wouldn't go into Pilate's court so that they would not be unclean. The reason they couldn't enter the Roman dwelling before was that they would not be able to perform their duties to offer the sacrifices or to properly celebrate the Passover because they could not become ceremonially clean again before the time established to sacrifice the Passover lamb. After the first day, however, being clean before supper wouldn't be an issue, as they could easily wash their selves from the uncleanness of touching something made unclean by someone else and be clean again at sunset to continue the feast (cf. "unclean" in Lev 22:5-7).

In all cases, the day following the day of preparation would be e(x-2) to m(x-2), and given that the chief priests and Pharisees went to talk with Pilate, this Scripture appears to be during the morning period after the m(x-3) crucifixion making this m(x-2).

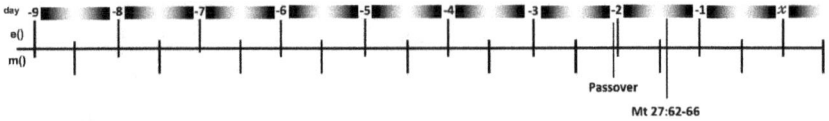

At this point, the narratives of the gospels all go silent. We have no recorded history from m(x-2) all the way to e(x). All is quiet until the late evening hours on the day of the resurrection. Remember, evening comes before morning, so when you read "the late evening hours" we are talking about the time just before sunrise.

| Mk 16:1-2 | "And when the sabbath was past, Mary Magdalene, and Mary the [mother] of James, and Salome, had bought sweet spices, that they might come and anoint him. ² And very early in the morning the first [day] of the week, they came unto the sepulchre at the rising of the sun." |

The word "had bought" is (ἀγοράζω – agorazō) and is in the aorist tense, active voice and indicative mood. This structure in the Greek does not identify the action as directly related to any other action; it only shows the action happened. To make a definitive decision on when the purchase happened (before Jesus' death, after His death, on the morning of His resurrection) would be unsubstantiated without the whole account to give the time. Mark offers inconclusive use and vocabulary in his gospel to determine when the purchase occurred, meaning we must seek for more context to decide.

The chapter markings were not part of Mark's gospel when written, and we do well to ignore them in historical reading such as this so that we don't lose the story as it unfolds. This verse makes more sense at the end of the previous chapter where it would read as follows beginning at Mk 15:46:

> And he [Joseph of Arimathea] bought fine linen, and
> took him down and wrapped him in the linen, and
> laid him in a sepulcher which was hewn out of a
> rock, and rolled a stone unto the door of the

74

sepulcher. [47] And Mary Magdalene and Mary the mother of Joses beheld where he was laid. [1] And when the sabbath was past, Mary Magdalene, and the mother of James and Salome, had bought sweet spices, that they might come and anoint him [2] And very early in the morning the first [day] of the week, they came unto the sepulchre at the rising of the sun. (Mk 15:46-16:2).

Seeing this in linear form as it was written, we see that Joseph of Arimathea made purchase leading up to Jesus' burial and so did the ladies. The account doesn't specifically suggest that the spices were purchased that morning before they went to the tomb, and the interaction in Lk 23:56 substantiates this understanding.

Also, their going to the tomb happened early in the morning (πρωΐ -- proi) which is the 4th watch of the night between the 9th hour and the 12th hour of the evening, which equated during that time of year to roughly between 4:30AM and 7:30AM. This then is on e(x) just before sunrise.

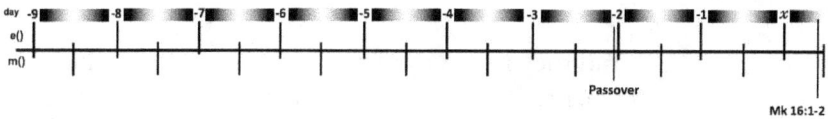

Mk 16:1-2

Mt 28:1   **"In the end of the sabbath, as it began to dawn toward the first [day] of the week, came Mary Magdalene and the other Mary to see the sepulchre. "**

The phrase "as it began to dawn" in the Greek (*epiphōskō*) means "to grow light," which equates to "before sunrise." This is stating that the Sabbath feast has ended and the next day is now reaching sunrise. This would be e(x) meaning after sunset and before sunrise as they are on the way to the tomb.

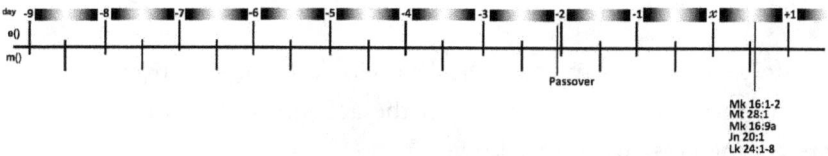

Mk 16:1-2
Mt 28:1
Mk 16:9a
Jn 20:1
Lk 24:1-8

Mk 16:9a   "Now when [Jesus] was risen early the first [day] of the week, he appeared first to Mary Magdalene, out of whom he had cast seven devils."

When Jesus was risen early. This is the Greek word (πρωΐ -- proi) which signifies before sunrise, so this is e(x).

Jn 20:1   "The first [day] of the week cometh Mary Magdalene early, when it was yet dark, unto the sepulchre, and seeth the stone taken away from the sepulchre."

At daybreak – before sunrise making this still evening. So, this is e(x)—the evening of the resurrection.

Lk 24:1-8   "Now upon the first [day] of the week, very early in the morning, they came unto the sepulchre, bringing the spices which they had prepared, and certain [others] with them."

Continuing on…

> ² And they found the stone rolled away from the sepulchre. ³ And they entered in, and found not the body of the Lord Jesus. ⁴ And it came to pass, as they were much perplexed thereabout, behold, two men stood by them in shining garments: ⁵ And as they were afraid, and bowed down [their] faces to the earth, they said unto them, Why seek ye the living among the dead? ⁶ He is not here, but is risen: remember how he spake unto you when he was yet in Galilee, ⁷ Saying, The Son of man must be delivered into the hands of sinful men, and be crucified, and the third day rise again. ⁸ And they remembered his words….

Very early in the morning, at daybreak (ὄρθρος – orthros), which is before morning. So, this piece of the account is still on e(x), but we are getting close to sunrise now.

Lk 24:9-11   **"And [the ladies] returned from the sepulchre, and told all these things unto the eleven, and to all the rest."**

Continuing…

> [10] It was Mary Magdalene, and Joanna, and Mary [the mother] of James, and other [women that were] with them, which told these things unto the apostles. [11] And their words seemed to them as idle tales, and they believed them not.

Here in Lk 24 as well as in Mt 28:1-10 and Mk 16:1-11 we find Mary Magdalene, Joanna, Mary the mother of Jesus, and "other women" going to the tomb who then come back and tell the disciples that Jesus was risen from the dead. Mark identifies Salome as one of the ladies as well. Starting with verse nine, it would now be m(x) because it is now after sunrise when the ladies return to tell their pre-sunrise experience to the disciples.

Mk 16:9b-13   **"Now when [Jesus] was risen early the first [day] of the week, he appeared first to Mary Magdalene, out of whom he had cast seven devils. [10] [And] she went and told them that had been with him, as they mourned and wept."**

Continuing…

> [11] And they, when they had heard that he was alive, and had been seen of her, believed not. [12] After that he appeared in another form unto two of them, as they walked, and went into the country. [13] And they went and told [it] unto the residue: neither believed they them."

On the first day of the week, Sunday morning, Jesus appears to: Mary Magdalene before sunrise, then to two others on the road in the countryside after sunrise, then later that morning to the eleven remaining apostles. Mark 16:9 identifies these events as happening the same daylight time period as the ladies seeing Jesus at the tomb and subsequently telling the disciples their experience. This would be $m(x)$, almost positively extending well into $e(x+1)$.

Lk 24:13,18,33   **"And, behold, two of them went that same day to a village called Emmaus, which was from Jerusalem [about] threescore furlongs…"**

Continuing…

> [18] And the one of them, whose name was Cleopas, answering said unto him, Art thou only a stranger in Jerusalem, and hast not known the things which are come to pass there in these days? … [33] And they rose up the same hour, and returned to Jerusalem, and found the eleven gathered together, and them that were with them…."

Cleopas and another man spend day with Jesus walking to Emmaus; Jesus expounds the gospel; eats with them late in the day (v. 29) and then vanishes. The distance was 60 furlongs from Jerusalem to Emmaus, which is 7.5 miles. They walked the entire way with Jesus, not knowing who He was, and then turned around after supper when they realized it was Him, and walked back. I estimate it would take 2½ - 2¾ hours each way, not including time for dinner preparations, so they likely returned to the upper room between 9:30PM and 11:30PM. This conversation and their experience with Jesus would be sometime between $m(x)$ to $e(x+1)$ with their return most definitely ending in $e(x+1)$.

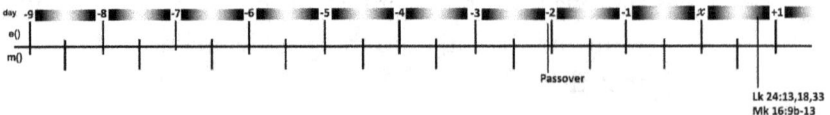

Lk 24:13,18,33
Mk 16:9b-13

Lk 24:36-49   "And as they thus spake, Jesus himself stood in the midst of them, and saith unto them, Peace [be] unto you."

Jesus stood among the disciples after His resurrection. It was the evening that Cleopas had returned from Emmaus after 9:30PM. This is e(x+1).

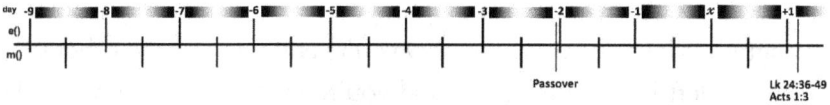

Acts 1:3,12   "To whom also he shewed himself alive after his passion by many infallible proofs, being seen of them forty days, and speaking of the things pertaining to the kingdom of God:"

Continuing…

> 12 Then returned they unto Jerusalem from the mount called Olivet, which is from Jerusalem a sabbath day's journey.

Jesus is with the disciples for 40 days. Starting m(x) on the first day of the week and going 40 days would make it a Friday morning when Jesus is taken up. It may reference a "sabbath day's journey" to dispel any concerns about them traveling back after Jesus ascension, as they may have walked back after sunset or while the sun was setting. This would be from m(x) to m(x+39).

Where Are We?

You're officially done examining all the large Scripture sections. Congratulations! All we have left are a few groups of smaller Scriptures and you will have digested the entire account from all four gospels. At the end, we'll summarize the story of the Passover, crucifixion and resurrection as we've discovered it, but there are Scriptures dealing with the resurrection that were not covered yet and which we examine in groups that follow. These are specifically the "three day" Scriptures, of which there are many. The Holy Spirit evidently felt strongly about the three-day aspect of Jesus' death and resurrection because it is the driving focus of the gospel accounts and the reason for this book. Before reading the conclusion of this study, please become familiar with these three-day Scriptures.

You're getting close to completion! You've been using your machete to cut through the jungle, you've been fighting your way through the vines and trees and now you're emerging on the other side. All that is left is some tall grass and you're in the clearing. Make the final push, because the treasure is within reach.

As a reminder and point of celebration for all the ground you've covered so far, the next page contains a diagram that shows you the relative day for each Scripture we've examined from m(x-9) when Jesus ate at Mary, Martha and Lazarus' house through His resurrection and appearing. You've come a long way! You should be proud of yourself.

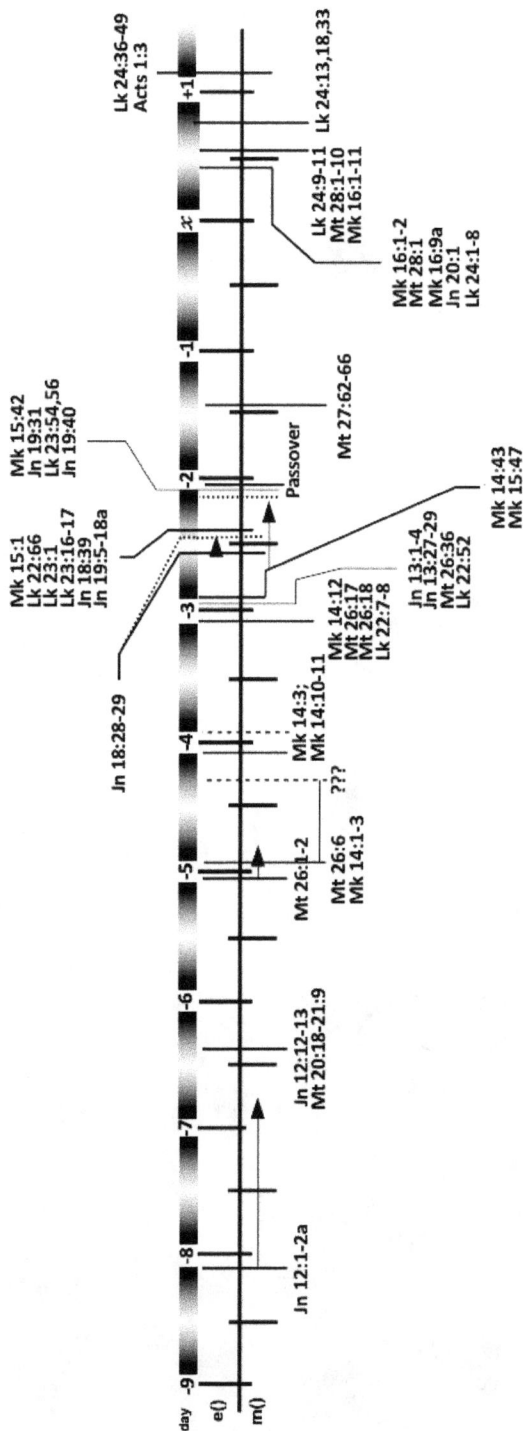

Chapter End Notes/Observations

THREE DAY LEARNING

J udaism, as other eastern cultures, often counts days beginning with the day one is on and then adding subsequent days moving forward: tallies may include part as well as whole days in the total depending on the context. Day tallies may also be bounded (having defined start and stop points) or cumulative (having a beginning and then adding to it). To understand the various three days scriptures, we need to examine the different types used in the biblical accounts. The following Scriptures all deal with Jesus and various three-day(s) Scriptures. When we group them together by kind, we observe four groups of Scriptures discussing the "3rd day", "three days", "three days and three nights" and "after three days." Consider the following.

Three Days (and Three Nights)

Of all the prophecies, the three days (and three nights) prophecies are the most definitive for the timeline of Jesus' death and resurrection. Consider the following Scriptures that represent each usage (duplicates between gospels are not included):

Mt 12:40   **"For as Jonas was three days and three nights in the whale's belly; so shall the Son of man be three days and three nights in the heart of the earth."**

Jn 2:19   **"Jesus answered and said unto them, Destroy this temple, and in three days I will raise it up."**

Mk 14:58   **"We heard him say, I will destroy this temple that is made with hands, and within three days I will build another made without hands."**

The Three Days Scriptures and the one Three Days and Three Nights Scripture follow the logic of a bounded set. A day is an evening and a morning combination as described by Genesis. So, within the combination of (in) three evenings and three mornings, these must occur.

To understand this, begin with the premise that Jesus died on Thursday during the 9th hour, which is between 2:45PM and 3:50PM. Using m( ) to represent morning (sunrise to sunset) and e( ) to represent evening (sunset to sunrise) so that the evening and the morning are a day and using "y" to represent the day Jesus was crucified, we then have the following sequence of grave time: m(y), e(y+1), m(y+1), e(y+2), m(y+2) and e(y+3). This equates to Jesus dying and in the grave before sunset Thursday [m(y)]; continuing in the grave after sunset Thursday (which now begins Friday) and before sunrise Friday [e(y+1)]; continuing in the grave after sunrise Friday and before sunset Friday [m(y+1)] (which now begins Saturday); continuing in the grave after sunset Friday and before sunrise Saturday [e(y+2)]; continuing after sunrise Saturday and before sunset Saturday [m(y+2)] (which now begins Sunday); and continuing in the grave after sunset Saturday and before sunrise Sunday [e(y+3)] at which point, before sunrise Sunday, Jesus was resurrected. This explains the fulfillment of the three days and three nights Scripture since there are three sunrise-to-sunset periods [m(y), m(y+1), m(y+2)] and three sunset-to-sunrise periods [e(y+1), e(y+2) and e(y+3)] in succession. It also fulfills the three days prophecy since Genesis states the summation of the evening and morning equal one day; and there are three pairs of mornings and evenings, again, in succession. These Scriptures only support a Thursday afternoon, before nightfall, death if Jesus is to be resurrected before sunrise on the first day of the week.

Third Day

Third is an ordinal position, meaning it depends on a position in a sequence based on some predetermined starting point as third requires a first and a second and the first is not the starting point, but the instant before the first is the starting point, and we are in the first until it is completed. When dealing with ordinal positions in Scripture, it appears we are to start on a date and accumulate time periods moving forward. A detailed conversation about this happens after these verses.

Mt 16:21   "From that time forth began Jesus to shew unto his disciples, how that he must go unto Jerusalem, and suffer many things of the elders and chief priests and scribes, and be killed, and be raised again the third day."

Mt 17:23   "And they shall kill him, and the third day he shall be raised again. And they were exceeding sorry."

Mt 20:19   "And shall deliver him to the Gentiles to mock, and to scourge, and to crucify [him]: and the third day he shall rise again."

Mt 27:64   "Command therefore that the sepulchre be made sure until the third day, lest his disciples come by night, and steal him away, and say unto the people, He is risen from the dead: so the last error shall be worse than the first."

Mk 9:31   "For he taught his disciples, and said unto them, The Son of man is delivered into the hands of men, and they shall kill him; and after that he is killed, he shall rise the third day."

Mar 10:34   "And they shall mock him, and shall scourge him, and shall spit upon him, and shall kill him: and the third day he shall rise again."

Luk 9:22   "Saying, The Son of man must suffer many things, and be rejected of the elders and chief priests and scribes, and be slain, and be raised the third day."

Luk 18:33   "And they shall scourge [him], and put him to death: and the third day he shall rise again."

Luk 24:7	"Saying, The Son of man must be delivered into the hands of sinful men, and be crucified, and the third day rise again."
Luk 24:21	"But we trusted that it had been he which should have redeemed Israel: and beside all this, to day is the third day since these things were done."
Luk 24:46	"And said unto them, Thus it is written, and thus it behoved Christ to suffer, and to rise from the dead the third day:"
Jhn 2:1	"And the third day there was a marriage in Cana of Galilee; and the mother of Jesus was there:"
Act 10:40	"Him God raised up the third day, and shewed him openly;"
1Co 15:4	"And that he was buried, and that he rose again the third day according to the scriptures"

While some might argue that the "third day" Scriptures are covered by the "three days" logic, I want to offer a different understanding.

The third day is ordinal, meaning it has a position, so we must ask, "…from what?" In Mt 16:21 it states, "be killed and be raised again the third day." The anchor experience is the understanding of "killed" and that is when the counting starts. The first day is the celebration of the completion of the first day since the anchor experience. The second day is the celebration of the completion of the second day since the anchor experience and the third day is the celebration of the third day of completion since the anchor experience.

We find a specific "third day" example from the book of John. Consider the following sequence: the anchoring event is when John begins ministry and is questioned about his origin (Jn 1:20-28); then in verse 29 "The next day John seeth Jesus coming unto him, and saith, Behold the Lamb of God, which taketh away the sin of the world" and "Again the next day [meaning the same day as v. 29] after John stood, and two of his disciples…"; then in verse 43 "The day following Jesus would go forth into Galilee, and findeth Philip, and saith unto him, Follow me"; and finally in Jn 2:1, "And the third day there was a marriage in Cana of Galilee; and the mother of Jesus was there…." So, it starts in v. 20; advances a day in vv. 29,35; another day in v.43 and reaches the 3rd day in Jn 2:1.

Next, consider Lev. 23:39 which illustrates,

> Also in the fifteenth day of the seventh month, when ye have gathered in the fruit of the land, ye shall keep a feast unto the LORD seven days: on the first day [shall be] a sabbath, and on the eighth day [shall be] a sabbath.

Moses notes the celebration is seven days, however he counts from the first as a starting point (not including the whole) to the eighth as the ending point to create seven full days. The only way this makes sense is if one starts with the first date as a beginning point (during the day for example when the sacrifices would be made) and begins to accrue morning/evening combinations until the final day of the celebration is reached. Here, then, one would count like this—from the morning sacrifice of the first to the morning sacrifice of the second is one day, from the morning sacrifice of the second to the morning sacrifice of the third is the second day…from the morning sacrifice of the sixth to the morning sacrifice of the seventh is the sixth day and from the morning sacrifice of the seventh to the morning sacrifice of the eighth is the seventh day of the feast but the eighth day in the sequence. Note, he's not saying the eighth day of the month which would be a bounded absolute reference, he is stating an accrued amount of time from a starting point. So, the question with the "third day" Scriptures is "the third day from what?"

The Jewish hour carries the same idea. The halachic hour[vi] (the hour as derived from Jewish religious practice) is 1/12 of the daylight in any given day. When the sun rises, you immediately enter the first hour, you don't start with the zeroth hour as there is no zeroth hour. It's not that you must complete an hour to call it "one," you are in the hour you call "one" while living it. This is different than saying "one o'clock" which means "when the hand reaches one on the clock." In the "one o'clock" mindset, you have already finished the full first hour (from 12 to 1) and you're now past it and beginning the second hour. Western culture says "one o'clock" but that is the celebration of the completion of the hour and we are already out of it by the time we call it so. But in the halachic hour, when you complete the first hour, you enter the second hour just as its starting, and you call it the second hour. When the Scriptures say the third hour, it means the span of time beginning at the end of the second fully completed hour and spanning through the third fully completed hour. This is much like saying something happened in the third century (years 201-300). The first century is 1-100. The second century is 101-200. The third century is 201-300. You live in the third century while it is happening.

So, consider the verse, "Now from the sixth hour there was darkness over all the land unto the ninth hour" (Mt 27:45). The "sixth unto the ninth" hour began at the close of the 5th hour and went through the conclusion and fulfillment of the 8th hour.

With this in mind, the third day for the resurrection would start with death on Thursday before sunset and would accrue two days and enter the "third" day. Death happening on Thursday at the 9th hour establishes the anchor point. So, Thursday from the 9th hour to Friday on the 9th hour is the first day; Friday at the 9th hour to Saturday at the 9th hour is the second day; Saturday at the 9th hour until Sunday at the 9th hour constitutes the conclusion of the third day. For a Scripture to meet the "third day" prophecy, it must be in that final e( ) to m( ) timeframe of the third day, in the case of the resurrection between e(x) and the conclusion of m(x), or in Gregorian terms, after Saturday at sunset and before Sunday at sunset.

Luke 13:32 is worth additional conversation.

Luk 13:32   "And he said unto them, Go ye, and tell that fox, Behold, I cast out devils, and I do cures to day and to morrow, and the third [day] I shall be perfected."

This is noteworthy as it is the one outlier in 16 verses. The other 15 meet the criteria identified above. This verse is not detailed enough to make a dissenting argument, because Jesus is speaking in a parable to Herod. Jesus says, "I cast out devils, and I do cures today and tomorrow…." To take this literally as a Scripture with which to count days, you would have to accept that Jesus stopped doing these things after "to morrow." We know this is not the case. We also know he was doing these things before this conversation. Jesus was using a parable to state, "I will do what I'm sent here to do until I'm done, and when I surrender my life for humanity, I will raise in a resurrected body on the third day."

After 3 Days

The following are the only two Scriptures identifying "after three days":

Mt 27:63　　**"Saying, Sir, we remember that that deceiver said, while he was yet alive, After three days I will rise again."**

Mk 8:31　　**"And he began to teach them, that the Son of man must suffer many things, and be rejected of the elders, and [of] the chief priests, and scribes, and be killed, and after three days rise again."**

The phrase "after three days" is processual and accruing (i.e. "after"). Recall that Jewish accumulation of days may include the anchor day itself, so if Thursday before sunset is the anchor, after three days would be: till sunset Thursday as the first day because we count the day we are on, till sunset Friday as the second day and till sunset Saturday as the third day…meaning sometime after sunset Saturday, as we enter Sunday, the event must occur.

The following section on the "after three days" Scriptures isn't necessary, but it may make more sense to consider an alternate view. There aren't many references in the New Testament of the word "after" being used in relation to accrued time, especially with enough context to fully determine the bounding of the timeframe. However, Lk 22:59 is an example of the word "after" being used in a timeframe:

> And about the space of one hour after another confidently affirmed, saying, Of a truth this [fellow] also was with him: for he is a Galilaean.

Here we see the following: a starting point (Peter denying Jesus the second time), the accumulation of time with the identifier of "about the space of an hour after," and the final outcome (realizing He'd betrayed Jesus). The phrase doesn't have accurate meaning without a beginning point, and from that beginning point, after accruing about an hour, an event occurred.

Another example is Act 15:33:

> And after they had tarried [there] a space, they were let go in peace from the brethren unto the apostles.

They began their tarrying and after an accrued time were let go. They came to Antioch (v. 30), they tarried in Antioch a space, they were let go.

Another example of the accrual understanding is Tit 3:10:

> A man that is an heretic after the first and second admonition reject....

Here again, we see the sequence of beginning point, accrual of time, and a concluding position which are: a man is identified as a heretic, he is corrected twice, he is rejected as a heretic. This is different than the sequential Scriptures where an event happens and the next item in sequence follows, here that would equate to a general statement declaring: after a heretic is identified, reject him.

The "after three days" Scriptures are not like the Scriptures that state "after" as in consequence to something. For example, consider Acts 20:6:

> And we sailed away from Philippi after the days of unleavened bread, and came unto them to Troas in five days; where we abode seven days.

After the days of unleavened bread" is a statement expressing sequence, not accrual of time.

Other examples of "after" as a sequence instead of time accrual can be seen here:

- "But after I am risen again, I will go before you into Galilee." – Mat 26:32
- "And came out of the graves after his resurrection, and went into the holy city, and appeared unto many." – Mat 27:53
- "But in those days, after that tribulation, the sun shall be darkened, and the moon shall not give her light…." – Mar 13:24

The accrual verses follow this pattern: a beginning point is named, an accrual of time occurs, after the accrual a concluding position is reached. The sequential Scriptures follow this pattern: an event happens and after that an occurrence follows.

With this understanding in hand, and remembering that eastern time-tracking methods may count the day an event occurs as the first day and then accrue from that point forward, we end up with Jesus dying on the afternoon of day 1, in the grave all of day 2, in the grave all of day 3 and resurrecting on day 4, which according to the Scripture is before sunrise on the first day of the week and is after three days.

Chapter End Notes/Observations

ARE WE FINISHED YET?

At this point, you may be tempted to jump to the conclusion of the book and be thinking, "I just want to know what happened." I hope you don't, because the next sections are golden, in my opinion. The purpose of this study is to help you wrap your mind around the events so that you can know with certainty the things you believe. I hope you'll continue to read the next few pages before the final conclusion where we unwrap the entire Passover and crucifixion account as it happened. It will likely be the first time in your life that you've read it this way, and your labor and study will be well rewarded. Keep going, you're near the prize!

Evening and Morning Functions as Days

In the following chart, resurrection is represented by (x) in the sequence of events, and all other dates are a function of adding or subtracting from that known day in the sequence of events. By now, you're a pro. The reason I didn't tell you about the chart early on was because you needed to get the functions firmly established in your mind. However, now, you may find it a helpful aid instead of a crutch.

As you review the chart, the columns labeled "day," "begin" and "end" are the apparent days in the month of Nisan on which the events happened. The day column is derived by laying the e( ) and m( ) outcomes from the Scripture accounts of the Passover, crucifixion and resurrection over the top of a linear calendar and sliding them left and right as a group until they all lineup with the restrictions of Scripture, the Jewish culture, and the lawful feast mandates and prohibitions.

For example, we know that Nisan 14 at evening is the Passover lamb sacrifice so the Passover dinner will not be where the Passover participants are eating this meal in the afternoon. We know that Nisan 15 is the first day of the Feast of Unleavened Bread, so we know it cannot fall on a day where people are recorded as doing any work other than cooking, since the Jews are commanded by God to "do no servile" work on the first day or the last day of the Feast of Unleavened Bread. We know that the priests and Sanhedrin cannot do anything considered work on a Sabbath day and are under walking distance restrictions and told to "stay put" on the Sabbath day as well. Once all e( ) and m( ) assignments are made from the gospel narrative, there appears to be only one way they can all line up with the Jewish feast calendar, where all prophecy is fulfilled, and where the Jewish law is honored and upheld by the priests and other Jewish leaders.

The gray row in the table below represents the timeframe in which Jesus was resurrected; all other time frames are either before that pivotal period (include a negative number of time periods) or after that pivotal period (include a positive number of time periods). Descriptions for the time periods are in the Begin and End columns.

Day	Function	Begin	End
N18	m(x+1)	After sunrise Monday	Before sunset Monday
N18	e(x+1)	After sunset Monday	Before sunrise Monday
N17	m(x)	After sunrise Sunday	Before sunset Sunday
N17	e(x)	After sunset Saturday	Before sunrise Sunday
N16	m(x-1)	After sunrise Saturday	Before sunset Saturday
N16	e(x-1)	After sunset Friday	Before sunrise Saturday
N15	m(x-2)	After sunrise Friday	Before sunset Friday
N15	e(x-2)	After sunset Thursday	Before sunrise Friday
N14	m(x-3)	After sunrise Thursday	Before sunset Thursday PSAC~<SSET[1]
N14	e(x-3)	After sunset Wednesday	Before sunrise Thursday
N13	m(x-4)	After sunrise Wednesday	Before sunset Wednesday
N13	e(x-4)	After sunset Tuesday	Before sunrise Wednesday
N12	m(x-5)	After sunrise Tuesday	Before sunset Tuesday
N12	e(x-5)	After sunset Monday	Before sunrise Tuesday
N11	m(x-6)	After sunrise Monday	Before sunset Monday
N11	e(x-6)	After sunset Sunday	Before sunrise Monday
N10	m(x-7)	After sunrise Sunday	Before sunset Sunday
N10	e(x-7)	After sunset Saturday	Before sunrise Sunday
N9	m(x-8)	After sunrise Saturday	Before sunset Saturday
N9	e(x-8)	After sunset Friday	Before sunrise Saturday
N8	m(x-9)	After sunrise Friday	Before sunset Friday

[1]PSAC~<SSET means "Passover sacrifice just before sunset"

Chapter End Notes/Observations

TRYING TO DISPROVE THE OUTCOME

By this point in the study, if you've arrived at the same conclusion as me, you believe the crucifixion must have happened on Thursday and not Friday. So, it was at this point that I turned my attention to the work of disproving a Thursday crucifixion. To disprove the Thursday event, I took all the historical accounts above and placed them on a timeline and marked the events that could not have happened because of Jewish law or another kind of restriction. I was curious to see how many possible crucifixion days of the week existed. After all, if I believed Thursday was the day and I could disprove Thursday, it couldn't be the correct day, right? I also wondered how many other week days would fit the chronology of events. The purpose of research is to disprove it. If we cannot disprove it, we have much more reason to believe we understand the truth.

Following are a series of images. I will label each one and below the first two images, I will list the items that cause the scenario to fail. The scenario we are trying to disprove is the day the crucifixion occurred. I understand that you won't be able to read all the entries in the cells, but suffice it to say that if you take all the e( ) and m( ) times we've defined from the gospel accounts and that you wrote on the upper right corner of your pages or cards, and if you order them starting with m(x-9) in descending chronological order so that you make a timeline out of them, you could then look for discrepancies as I did, and here is what you would see. Depending on the format of book you're reading, you may see shades of gray or specific colors. Watch for the following highlights that carry specific meaning: Red/Dark Gray (DG) = Doesn't fulfill the 3days/3nights prophecy; Yellow/Light Gray (LG) = Conflicts with Jewish practices; Pink/Medium Gray (MG) = Odd circumstances that don't make sense in that scenario—may or may not be wrong.

Friday Crucifixion

For a Friday crucifixion:

- Jn 12:1-2a – Pink/MG – Jesus would have walked to Mary, Martha and Lazarus' house on the Sabbath day and had supper with them as the first meal on Sunday. It is unlikely this would happen on Sabbath feast as Jesus walked to their house on this day for the supper. He would have been under Sabbath walking restrictions which means no more than ½ of a mile by estimate. Jesus had resorted to a village called Ephraim toward the wilderness before coming to this dinner, which is now called Taybeh and is about nine miles from Bethany. This is well beyond a sabbath day's walk. Further, Mary, Martha and Lazarus would have been under restriction for meal preparation, and Mary could not have worked to anoint Jesus without breaking the Sabbath feast laws.
- Deut 16:5-6 – Yellow/LG – The Passover sacrifice happens at the going down of the sun on the 14th of Nisan. If this were the Passover sacrifice day, it would be after the 9th hour and before the end of the 12th hour. Jesus is our Passover lamb (1 Cor 5:7). For Jesus to offer Himself on Friday does not allow for a 3-day/3-night resurrection on the first day of the week.

His death on a Friday would only provide Friday, Saturday night, Saturday morning, Sunday night making a total of two days and two nights

- Mk 16:9a – Red/DG – Jesus was risen early the first day of the week; this could not have happened and fulfilled the 3-day/3-night prophecy if He died on Friday.

- Lk 23:54,56 – Pink/MG – Jesus' body is laid in the grave and "that day was the preparation and the sabbath drew on." This statement is illogical..."and the sabbath drew on." The presence of the phrase signifies it was beyond immediate reach, hence "...drew on." That is not the case when the Sabbath is a few hours from the event.

- Mt 27:62 – Pink/MG – The chief priests and pharisees come to Pilate and ask the tomb be sealed. It is highly unlikely as the priests would have defiled the Sabbath by breaking the walking laws. It is further unlikely that they would have left their Passover celebrations and families, much less the command to "stay put" in order to do this.

Saturday Crucifixion

For a Saturday crucifixion:

- Jn 13:1-4 – Yellow/LG – Jesus rises from supper (not Passover) which is the beginning of the Sabbath feast. He would have then washed the disciple's feet. This cannot be due to the Sabbath restrictions.

- Jn 18:28-29 – Yellow/LG – Jesus is taken to Pilate. Could not happen without breaking the Sabbath laws.

- Jn 13:27-29 – Yellow/LG – Judas leaves Jesus and the disciples at the feast in the evening and goes to betray him. Cannot be due to the Sabbath restrictions.

- Mt 26:36 – Yellow/LG – Jesus goes to Gethsemane with the disciples. Cannot be due to the Sabbath restrictions and because He would have broken the Passover celebration law.

- Jesus is our Passover lamb (1 Cor 5:7) – Red/DG – Gospel accounts are plain that the Jewish leaders want Jesus dead before the feast. Jesus' death on Wednesday or before does not allow for a 3-day/3-night resurrection on the first day of the week.

- His death on a Saturday – Pink/MG – would not create 24 hours before His resurrection or would create a week to reach the next one

- Lk 22:52 – Yellow/LG – In Gethsemane, Jesus addresses the chief priests, captains of the temple and elders. Cannot be due to the Sabbath restrictions.

- Mk 15:42 – Red/DG – Joseph of Arimathea asks for Jesus' body. This is the day of crucifixion and based on the Jonah prophecy must be three days before Jesus' resurrection so as the first of three m( ) periods required to fulfill that prophecy.

- Mk 14:43 – Yellow/LG – Judas comes to kiss Jesus in Gethsemane. Cannot be due to the Sabbath work and walk restrictions because Judas should be with his family.

- Jn 19:31 – Yellow/LG – the Jews sought that the legs of the crucified would be broken so that they would die before the preparation, and by account, before the Passover since the rulers wanted to do it before the feast days and that would make the preparations happen on the Sabbath which wasn't possible.

- Lk 23:54,56 – Pink/MG – Jesus' body is laid in the grave and "that day was the preparation and the sabbath drew on." This would not happen on a Sabbath day since it would be the same day and would not need to "draw on."

- Jn 18:39 – Pink/MG – Pilate offers to release Jesus. This would likely not happen on a Sabbath feast. There is no further preparation that needs to happen, but the account of Jesus' death states that the Sabbath was approaching. For it to be a week away is unlikely since the Sabbath had just occurred in this scenario. Further, it is extremely unlikely that the first day of unleavened bread, Nisan 15, would start in the middle of Sabbath.

- Jn 19:5-18a – Yellow/LG – It was the preparation of the Passover and about the 6th hour. This would not happen on a Sabbath day.

- Lk 23:16-17 – Pink/MG – Pilate must release a prisoner (likely Nisan 14 since it's the day before the feast--interestingly, this is the morning after gethsemane). Not likely that Pilate would do this on a Sabbath feast day.

By now you get the idea…Here are the rest of the days of the week, each day with its problems highlighted…

Sunday Crucifixion

Monday Crucifixion

Tuesday Crucifixion

Wednesday Crucifixion

Thursday Crucifixion

The Thursday crucifixion is the only possible scenario that fulfills the entire Scripture account with just a two potential oddities listed below this image. These are questions and not inhibitors; the oddities are merely things we don't know for certain, not things that disqualify the day. All other days of the week have disqualifiers. Thursday does not.

- We don't know from Scripture why the disciples asked to prepare the Passover celebration a day earlier than the rest of Israel: this action doesn't invalidate the gospel accounts; we simply aren't told in the Scripture. However, this appears to be answered in the Mishnah and is covered in the section titled "Observation from the Mishnah."

- Mt 27:62 states the chief priests and pharisees come to Pilate and ask that the tomb be sealed. Because this is not yet Sabbath, the chief priests are not breaking Sabbath laws, and the conversation about sealing the tomb is likely not a breaking of the "no servile work" law because they coerced the Romans into doing the work their selves, telling them that if they allowed the disciples to steal the body, the situation would be worse than before. Even walking to the tomb is fine because they are not in the Sabbath feast (hence the "stay put" law doesn't apply) and they have already kept the Passover the night before and now only need to wash in water before evening to be clean again if they venture to visit a Roman dwelling. Given the scriptural narrative, it seems obvious that the Jewish rulers did not perceive these actions as breaking any Feast restrictions.

Chapter End Notes/Observations

EXTRA-BIBLICAL
OBSERVATIONS

The Scripture holds the sum total of all we need to observe about the crucifixion; I do not include this section to somehow prove the Scripture. You could skip this section and go straight to the chapter titled "The Scripture-only Conclusion" and it would be just as true whether you read the following information or not. There are a few non-essential curiosities the Scriptures don't hand us, and the following historical documents seemingly add some additional color.

Observations from the Mishnah

While the Mishnah is not the Scripture, it gives valuable background to what was happening in AD190 and centuries before. The website Sefaria states, "Composed in Talmudic Israel (c.190 - c.230 CE). Pesachim (Passover Festivals) belongs to the second order, Moed (Festivals) and discusses the prescriptions regarding the Passover and the paschal sacrifice. It has ten chapters."[vii] The Mishnah Pesachim records what was understood to be the defined practices of the Jews by AD190 as passed from rabbi to rabbi for myriad generations prior. While I won't use this data to justify a Thursday crucifixion—the gospels do that alone—I want you to see what may have been happening as the extra-biblical sources give food for thought.

Why a Day Before Everyone Else?

The gospel account points to Jesus and the disciples making their Passover preparations on the day before the rest of mainstream Israel, eating a meal together, leaving the meal to journey to the Garden of

Gethsemane, Jesus' arrest and crucifixion the subsequent afternoon, and all just before the Passover sacrifices occurred. The Scriptures are silent on why Jesus had a prior-day preparation and meal before Passover; however, the gospel writer, John, does specifically state that the meal Jesus ate with the disciples was *not* the Passover (Jn 13:1-4). Not knowing why Jesus ate this non-Passover meal doesn't affect its validity or potency: it's merely a question that remains silent in the gospels. However, the Mishnah offers a potential and intriguing explanation.

In Mishnah Pesachim chapter 4, the first Mishnah (equivalent to a verse) states that the combination of the most restrictive rules must be observed between people who travel from one place to another for the Passover celebration. If a person travels to a place that has more stringent practices to a place with looser practices, the more stringent should be followed. Conversely, if a person travels from a place with loose practices to a place that has restrictive ones, then the restrictive should still be followed. Consider this excerpt:

> In a place where it is the custom to do work on the
> eve of Pesah until midday one may do work; where it
> is the custom not to do work, one may not do work.
> He who goes from a place where they work to a
> place where they do not work, or from a place where
> they do not work to a place where they do work,
> they place upon him the restrictions of the place
> from where he departed and the restrictions of the
> place to where he has gone. And a man must not act
> differently [from local custom] on account of the
> quarrels [which would ensue].[viii]

And Mishnah 5 in chapter 4 states:

> In a place where it is the custom to do work on the
> ninth of Av, one may do it; where it is the custom
> not to do work, one may not do it. And in all places
> students of sages desist [from work on that day].
> Rabban Shimon ben Gamaliel said: a man should
> always make himself a student of sages. But the sages
> say: In Judea they used to do work on the eve of

> Pesah until midday, while in Galilee they did not
> work at all. [With regard to] the night: Beth Shammai
> forbid [work], but Bet Hillel permit it until sunrise.[ix]

Here, we see that there was an understood difference between Galilean Jews and other Jews. The Galilean Jews did no work on the standard preparation day the rest of Judaism would respect. This means that all Passover preparations had to occur the day before the normal day of preparation, even if traveling to an area where preparations were allowed until the end of the day just before the Passover sacrifice was made. It was understood that the person carries the most restrictive summary practice (most restrictive when compared between where the person came from and where they are) wherever they celebrate the Passover, since Mishnah Pesachim 4:1 states, "they place upon him the restrictions of the place from where he departed and the restrictions of the place to where he has gone...." Even without this practice of the most restrictive habit, people in Israel would not have judged Jesus or the disciples for preparing a day early, because cleansing rituals and the cleaning of dwellings took up to a week. It would have been different if they were preparing when everyone else was already celebrating.

According to Mishnah 5:4, Jesus and the disciples, being Galilean, would have kept the day-before Passover preparation while the non-Galileans would have kept the day-of preparations. But why? A possible solution to this question is a fast on the day of preparation known as a seudah hamafseket. It was long practiced and understood that the Fast of the Firstborn happened, and still happens, the day before Passover is celebrated in honor of the first born who were saved during the Exodus. This has been referenced in Talmudic (Jewish law and history) writings before AD200, signifying it has been a long-standing practice for the firstborn males of any family and of those who fast in memory of God's faithfulness to the firstborn. Here is a fascinating coincidence. If the meal Jesus ate with the disciples was a seudah hamafseket, we should then be calling it by its proper name. Seudah hamafseket, means "the final meal." Eaten in the evening, could this be where we've derived "the last supper?" Coincidence? Possibly.

Just as intriguing is the planning of God. Do you realize that if this is indeed true, and we have no reason to believe it is not, Jesus being Galilean worked to fulfill prophecy, not only about His birth, but His death as well? Gospel writer Matthew records a prophecy, "He shall be called a Nazarene" (Mt 2:23), and Nazareth is in Galilee. It seems the plan of God may have been to make Him a Nazarene to establish all that we have seen unfold. If he was not a Galilean, it is possible that He may not have prepared the formal meal the day before to eat with His disciples—the meal that used much of the Passover elements without being the Passover meal. Had this been the actual Passover meal, He could not have gone to the Garden of Gethsemane without breaking the Sabbath feast laws, nullifying Him as savior; we would not have the eucharist we do today which is open to Jew and gentile with no argument about feast laws; and much of the account may have looked different. As it is, God used Jesus' Galilean upbringing as part of His plan of redemption. It is amazing that God would place His Son in a country where the Passover preparations happened a day early, to potentially keep all the events in synch. I realize this is arguable because Jesus could still have had dinner the day before, but the fluidity with which all the events unfolded revolves partly around the fact that Jesus was a Galilean, and whether it had to happen that way or not, it did. It's just very interesting to see the nuance God invested in the redemption of mankind.

Priestly Uncleanness

Another question possibly illuminated by extra-biblical sources is an answer to the question about why the chief priests would not enter Pilate's home on the day of preparation. This interaction can be read in Mishnah Pesachim 7:7 where the Mishnah interacts with the cleanness of the worshipper who is making the Pascal sacrifice for his family:

> A pesah whose blood has been sprinkled and then it became known that it was unclean, the frontlet propitiates. If the body of [the owner] became unclean, the frontlet does not propitiate, because they [the sages] said: [in the case of] a nazirite, and he who sacrifices the pesah-offering, the frontlet propitiates for the uncleanness of the blood, but the

frontlet does not propitiate for the uncleanness of
the body [of the owner]. If he was defiled with the
uncleanness of the deep, the frontlet propitiates.[x]

The general understanding of this Mishnah is that if the men were
unclean, they could not offer their Passover sacrifice, and since the
simplest forms of uncleanness were mitigated by a ceremonial bath
before sunset, with cleansing coming only at and after sunset, because
the Passover lamb had to be sacrificed *before* sunset and then cooked
and eaten, they would have no time to wash and be clean before they
needed to make their offering, which would render their sacrifice
unclean. If the offering could have been made after sunset, this would
not have been an issue, but since the order would have been: priests
enter Pilate's home, priests become unclean, make their Passover
sacrificial offerings, wash at nightfall and *then* become clean, it would
have defiled their Passover sacrifices and made them unacceptable to
God.

The Length of the Passover Meal

We have adequate information in the Scripture that states the
Passover meal took all night, specifically, the book of Deuteronomy
(16:7) states that the meal would take until morning. Even so, it is
interesting to note what the Mishnah states in regard to the timing of
the Passover meal.

In Mishnah 10:1-8, we read:

> [1] On the eve of Pesah close to minhah one may not
> eat until nightfall. Even the poorest person in Israel
> must not eat [on the night of Pesah] until he reclines.
> And they should give him not less than four cups [of
> wine], and even from the charity plate.[xi]

And...

> [8] One may not conclude the pesah meal with an
> afikoman. If some of them fell asleep, they may eat
> [the pesah when they wake up]. If all of them fell
> asleep they may not eat. Rabbi Jose says: if they

napped, they may eat, but if they fell asleep, they may not eat.[xii]

The understood practice was that one would recline, have no less than four cups of wine and possibly nap during the event. All this suggests that as early as AD195, the understood practice passed from generation to generation was a long and relaxing meal, not a rushed meal where the participants would leave their home to travel to a garden for prayer in the middle of the night.

Time of Passover Offering and Jesus' Crucifixion

There is nothing in the Scripture that states what time of the day the Passover offerings were made other than in the evening. However, the Mishnah discusses this.

In Mishnah Pesachim 5:1, we read:

> The [afternoon] tamid is slaughtered at eight and a half hours and is offered at nine and a half hours. On the eve of Pesah it is slaughtered at seven and a half hours and offered at eight and a half hours, whether it is a weekday or Shabbat. If the eve of Pesah fell on the eve of Shabbat it is slaughtered at six and a half hours and offered at seven and a half hours, and the pesah offering after it.xiii

This paragraph identifies that the evening sacrifice happens at 8½ hours into the day[xiv]. This is listed in the Passover processes highlighted in Mishnah Pesachim 5:3, that discuss the Passover offering:

> ...If he slaughtered it before midday, it is disqualified, because it is said, "[and all of the assembled congregation of Israelites shall slaughter it] at twilight" (Exodus 12:6). If he slaughtered it before the [evening] tamid, it is fit, providing that a person stirs its blood until [that of] the tamid is sprinkled. [Nevertheless] if it was sprinkled [before the tamid], it is fit.[xv]

By reference, we see the expectation was that it would be sacrificed after the tamid (the morning or evening offering)[xvi]. The evening tamid was offered at the 8½ hour mark during Passover. Jesus died sometime after the 9th hour mark, meaning that Jesus offered Himself during the same hours that the rest of the nation of Israel was offering their individual Passover lamb sacrifices for all the homes of Israel.

Observations from the Gemara

While the Gemara (another authoritative piece of Jewish literature) is not the Mishnah, it has an interesting account that applies to the process of shrouding the dead. In the discussion found in Yevamot 66b:8, we read, "The Gemara relates an incident: A certain woman brought into her marriage to her husband a robe [itztela] of fine wool [meileta], which was deemed guaranteed property by her marriage contract. Her husband subsequently died, and the orphans took that robe and spread it over the corpse as a shroud. The woman demanded that the robe be returned to her."[xvii] In this example, we see the cloth was "spread…over" the corpse "as a shroud." This signifying that the cloth used was draped over an upward-facing individual who was laid as if resting or sleeping.[xviii]

In his explanation of Mishnah 3:8:2, Dr. Joshua Kulp explains:

> "Normally, the bier, a stretcher with the body on it,
> would be placed on the thruway, the central road
> that passes through the town, so that people would
> have the opportunity to offer up public eulogies."[xix]

The body would be covered with a shroud while on the bier. In Jesus' case, the process happened so quickly that His body hadn't been properly prepared, the proof of which is seen in these verses:

> And the women also, which came with him from
> Galilee, followed after, and beheld the sepulchre, and
> how his body was laid. And they returned, and
> prepared spices and ointments; and rested the
> sabbath day according to the commandment – Lk
> 23:55-56.

The women took note how His body was laid, likely because it wasn't right, and they knew they still had a job to complete.

Given all we observe in Scripture and in the Jewish texts, here is what I believe happened: Joseph of Arimathea and Nicodemus brought a stretcher to carry Jesus' body; they laid a large piece of cloth on the stretcher that was longer than two times Jesus' body; they applied some of the 100# bag of spices and aloes on the cloth, then had the Romans lay Jesus' body on the spiced cloth, being careful their selves not to touch Jesus; they applied more of the bag of spices and then covered Jesus by folding the cloth over the top of Him to shroud Him from shame as they walked through the streets. They then carried Jesus to the tomb where they laid Him on the burial slab, straightened out the cloths' ends out of respect to the dead, and left the tomb. To bring Jesus from the stretcher to the slab, they would have wound the corners of the cloth to make handles and used them to pull Jesus over to the place where He lay (an alternate possible meaning for "wound"). When done, they would then straighten and drape the cloth over Jesus like a sheet, not "wound around" him like a mummy since the Jews did not practice that type of burial winding and because they were expecting to come back and properly inter the body after the Sabbath feast was complete. This possible account would be consistent with the observations surrounding the Shroud of Turin[xx].

Observations from Josephus

The writings of Josephus are a great place to observe interactions between the Jews and Romans as they revolve around the day of preparation and Jesus' Roman trial. Here, we can see why Pilate was so intent to solve this case and move on. Note here the words of Flavius Josephus in his journal titled The Antiquity of the Jews (AD94), specifically what he notes in chapter 16:

> [163] it seemed good to me and my counselors, according to the sentence and oath of the people of Rome, that the Jews have liberty to make use of their own customs, according to the law of their forefathers, as they made use of them under Hyrcanus the high priest of the Almighty God; and that their sacred money be not touched, but be sent to Jerusalem, and that it be committed to the care of the receivers at Jerusalem; and that they be not

obliged to go before any judge on the Sabbath day, nor on the day of the preparation to it, after the ninth hour.

Pilate would have been most interested to honor Roman law by being done with the Jews trial before the 9th hour. As we know, Jesus was crucified on the 6th hour and died sometime after the 9th hour.

Chapter End Notes/Observations

CAN WE KNOW THE DATE?

Before we end with the final account as described by Scripture, as fantastic as this may seem, it appears possible to tell the year and date of Jesus' death. This is not presented as an argument and I'm not inviting battles over these observations. I merely offer them a fascinating outcome of this study.

Passover is the 14th day of the first month of the new Jewish calendar year. The first month of any new year is determined by the visibility of the first crescent after the vernal (Spring) equinox. When the crescent is visible, that becomes the first day of the first month. The first crescent of any new moon may be visible with the unaided eye just after the 15th hour of the new moon's existence depending on meteorological phenomena. If we evaluate all the possible dates for visible crescents after the spring equinox between AD26 and AD38 (the only times available during Jesus' possible ministry life), there is only one day in one year that offers a crescent moon possibly visible at a time that allows the Passover to happen at nightfall on the 14th day where that 14th day is a Thursday; that date is April 6, AD30. AD37 offers a Thursday possibility, however, it seems the full moon on that day happens too late to allow the visible crescent 13 days prior. Therefore, it appears nearly indisputable that Jesus our Passover sacrifice died for us on April 6, AD30 between 2:45PM and 3:50PM.[xxi]

FINAL PERSONAL THOUGHTS

This has been one of the most rewarding Scripture studies I've done. It illustrates that everything necessary to understand the Passover and resurrection account of Scripture is in the pages of the Gospels, if we allow them to speak. It illustrates that Jesus fulfilled the Passover obligations to the letter, so that when the Apostle Paul writes that Christ our Passover is sacrificed for us, he really meant that Jesus our Passover offering was indeed sacrificed for us. Our opportunity to see the Scripture self-define and prove the events of the passion week is life changing. To now understand the teaching I've received for years, based on church tradition, is lacking and to finally see the truth as outlined in Scripture, is beautiful and only prepares me to defend the gospel of Jesus that much more authoritatively. I'm grateful to God for the opportunity to see all that is here, and grateful for the fruit it will produce in any Jesus follower who takes the time to internalize the truth of the Passover, crucifixion and resurrection account. With my final personal thoughts complete, let's put all the pieces together and end with the scriptural account the way it appears to have happened as explained by all four gospels.

THE SCRIPTURE-ONLY CONCLUSION

Six days before the Passover celebration, Jesus is at Mary, Martha and Lazarus' house. He arrives on Friday evening just before supper begins and prepares to eat the Sabbath feast according to the law of Moses—this feast happens every week. It begins Friday night at sunset and is over at sunset the next day. While at Mary, Martha and Lazarus' house, He enjoys dinner and stays the day (which, remember is sunset to sunset) as people in close proximity (within a Sabbath day's walk) come and listen to him at their house. It is here at Lazarus' home that Jesus is first anointed. His feet are anointed by Mary the sister of Lazarus, and Jesus declares her actions as preparation for His burial, signifying to those near Him that He will not be properly interred at His death.

The next day following, at the end of the Sabbath feast and Jesus time in Bethany, which is now Sunday morning, Jesus goes into Jerusalem where people greet him with palms shouting "Hosanna!" This was legitimately Palm Sunday. This occurs on the 10th day of the first month (Nisan 10), which is the same day that the rest of Israel is finding their personal Passover sacrificial lamb and ushering it into their homes until it is sacrificed on the 14th day. The sacrifice was to live with each house in Israel until it was killed, roasted and consumed by the family. While the homes of Israel each usher in their sacrificial lamb, the nation of Israel as a whole is ushering in its sacrificial lamb.

Then, two days before the Passover, on a Tuesday, Jesus is at Simon the Leper's house. There, at a meal, He is anointed for burial a second time; this time His head is anointed. Again, Jesus states this is for His burial. Both now, and with Mary's anointing, Jesus is telling the disciples that He won't be properly interred. Jesus knows that after He dies and before the time people come back to the grave to prepare him properly for burial, He will be resurrected.

That night after supper at Simon's house as the narrative crosses from Tuesday to Wednesday, Judas goes to the priests and agrees to betray Jesus for payment, establishing an agreement to hand him over to the Jewish rulers who had already began conspiring among their selves how to kill Jesus.

The next day, Wednesday on the Gregorian calendar, which is the day before the Passover sacrifice is made at nightfall, Jesus sends Peter and John to the upper room to prepare for the Passover celebration with the mandate to tell the owner of the upper room, "Where is the room where we [my disciples and I] may or may not eat the Passover?" Jesus said it this way because He was aware that while the disciples would return to the upper room after the crucifixion to partake of the Passover and comfort each other, He would not be with them. This is now happening on Nisan 13, the day before the rest of Israel prepares for *their own* Passover meals. Note that Jesus has the disciples prepare for the Passover celebration a day earlier than the rest of Israel[xxii].

Once Peter and John are finished preparing for the Passover, the disciples meet Jesus in the upper room, and they all enjoy a meal together. John specifically records that this is *not* the Passover, and this is affirmed in multiple verses in all the gospels. Even though the disciples ate some of the items that would also be consumed the next day at the Passover meal, this was not the Passover meal. At the end, Jesus sends Judas out of the upper room and Judas goes to get the authorities while Jesus washes the disciples' feet and they go with Jesus to the garden of Gethsemane. Because this is not yet the Passover meal, Jesus is not breaking the feast laws established by God. Further, Jesus using a meal that was not the Passover meal as the foundation for communion removes all argument about the Jewish requirements for the celebration of the Eucharist for the soon-to-be-added, gentile church. This is now the evening of the 14th day (aka/ the beginning of Nisan 14). The end of this day is when the nation of Israel will sacrifice its Passover lamb toward the end of daylight.

Remember, by the end of today, we will begin the Passover meal and the first day of the Feast of Unleavened Bread, and that first feast day will fall on a Friday. However, this Friday is not a typical Friday. A typical Friday would be the preparation for the Sabbath feast, but this time, they had a problem: this Friday is the first day of the Feast of Unleavened Bread and there are restrictions that must be followed. Israel can do "no servile labor" this Friday, which means all they can do is cook in regard to work, because cooking is the only work that is allowed on the first and last days of the Feast of Unleavened Bread. This forces all Israel to do two days of preparation in one: preparation for the first day of the Feast of Unleavened Bread and simultaneously preparation for the Sabbath feast, because all the shopping and preparations cannot happen when they normally would. This is why the gospel writers expressed phrases like "and the sabbath drew on" when describing the expanse of time between the crucifixion and the actual Sabbath feast.

Jesus is arrested early on Nisan 14 (likely between the 6th and 9th hour of night, which would be between midnight and 3AM) and taken to Jerusalem where He stands trial before the Jews and then the Romans. By the 6th hour of the day (roughly noon), Jesus is crucified and then dies on Nisan 14 after the 9th hour, which during that time of year would have been after 2:45PM and before 3:50PM. This is the same time the entire nation of Israel is sacrificing their Passover lambs for each of their own homes: just in the last hours of daylight. Jesus, our Passover, offered Himself as the Passover sacrifice at the same time the rest of the Passover sacrifices were being offered for all Jewish families. Jesus dies and is on the cross for a period of time while Joseph of Arimathea goes to request His body from the Romans.

The Romans, after confirming Jesus is dead by spearing Him in the side, take His body down. The gospels record the phrase "as was the manner of the Jews" when referencing Jesus burial process, which means they would have laid Jesus body on a cloth draped over a stretcher. Joseph would have draped the body in cloth to hide Jesus from shame as he and another man take Jesus to the tomb where they twist the corners of the cloth as handles, drag him over to the bench that had been hewn from rock, straighten and drape the cloth over Him and roll the stone across the entrance. At this point, there is just enough light left that the women who accompanied His body note that Jesus' was not properly interred in the tomb and so they use the remaining light to go back to the upper room and prepare the spices they have already purchased and that they will take back after the Sabbath has passed. Because this is happening Thursday before sunset, that means the Passover meal, known as the first meal of the Feast of Unleavened Bread, begins as the first meal of Friday at sunset, just minutes after they return to the upper room. That night, all Israel is celebrating the Passover; the Jewish leaders are exalting in the fact that Jesus is now dead; the priests are trying to figure out how the temple veil tore from top to bottom; all are with their families and friends; and the disciples are all together, comforting each other in the upper room.

Since we are now into Friday, this is the first day of the Feast of Unleavened Bread, and is now the first feast day when God has declared that "no servile work" may be done. That means no work other than cooking, but without restrictions on walking: no "stay put" rule existed for the Feast of Unleavened Bread.

On that Friday morning, after they had completed their Passover meal requirements and before Sabbath begins that night at sunset, the priests become concerned about the disciples stealing Jesus' body and, because it is not yet the Sabbath feast, were able to go to the Romans to make certain that Jesus' body is guarded and the tomb sealed. Passover feast law did not restrict their conversations or their walking distances. The restriction was "no servile work." Because of this, they were able to go talk with the Romans and convince them to safeguard their decision by making the order to secure the tomb with a guard. The Jewish leaders walk to the tomb with the guard to see that it is secured and sealed by the Romans and then go home to their families for the Sabbath feast, which they had prepared with the rest of their Passover fixings the day before and were possibly now cooking on Friday.

Then, the gospels are silent until the end of the Sabbath.

So, Jesus was crucified on Thursday as the sun is setting. The Jews have the tomb guarded on Friday and they finish cooking their food for the Sabbath feast that same day. The ladies cannot work the day after Jesus' death because that is the first day of the Feast of Unleavened Bread, and they cannot work the day after that because it is then the Sabbath feast day. They cannot respond any further until after the third evening of Jesus' death and burial.

They arrive the first day of the week, Sunday, as the sun is rising and Jesus is missing. Jesus died Thursday afternoon before sunset which is m(x-3), He was in the tomb Friday morning m(x-2) and Saturday morning m(x-1). He was also in the tomb the Friday evening e(x-2), Saturday evening e(x-1), and Sunday evening e(x), which is the beginning of Sunday, during which time He was resurrected before the morning sunrise, fulfilling the three-day and three-night self-identified prophecy for the sign of Jonah.

That Sunday morning after sunrise, many disciples see Jesus. Cleopas and another walk with him for hours on the road to Emmaus without knowing who He was till the last minute. They make the 2¾ hour journey back to Jerusalem, and once regathered with the disciples, Jesus appears in the upper room where He eats fish and honeycomb with them on day two of the Feast of Unleavened Bread, fulfilling His words that He may or may not eat the Passover with the disciples: He didn't eat on day one, but He did on day two. He spends that day and the next 39 days thereafter with the disciples before ascending to God on a Friday and ten days after His ascension, in the same upper room because Jesus told them to tarry there in Jerusalem until they were given power from on high (Lk 24:49), the disciples are baptized in the Holy Spirit as Jesus said they would be—still in the same upper room where they ate their last supper with Him.

With this amazing account, the church age begins. This conclusion supports every gospel verse that discusses the Passover celebration, Jesus' crucifixion, death and resurrection, and is supported by all the gospels as well.

Chapter End Notes/Observations

APPENDIX A: EVENING AND MORNING AS FUNCTIONS

This handout gives you the chance to practice creating and interpreting the e( ) and m( ) functions we will use for the remainder of the study. See if you can properly answer the following evening and morning functions. This paper is self-checking. Don't cheat, but notice that the bottom half is just the top half re-written but taking out different words

e(x) the evening of _____

e(x-3) three evenings before the _____

m(x+3) three mornings after the _____

m(x-6) six _____ before the _____

m(x-16) _____ mornings _____ the _____

e(x+39) 39 _____ after the _____

e(x+39) 39 evenings _____ the resurrection

m(x-16) sixteen _____ before the resurrection

m(x-6) six mornings _____ the resurrection

m(x+3) three mornings _____the resurrection

e(x-3) three _____ before the resurrection

e(x) the evening of the resurrection

APPENDIX B: RESEARCHING POSSIBLE DATES OF NISAN 14

As you enter this section and consider my thoughts and findings, please realize that I am not an astronomer. There are myriad people who have knowledge and experience light years beyond my own. I began the process of trying to figure out when the earliest crescent moon would be visible and ended up coming to a completely different conclusion. That said, this section is not polished with an intent of convincing anyone of my skills. If anything, I'll likely embarrass myself by including it. Just the same, I consider myself an average person trying to discern the Scripture and I feel it may be useful to other normal people as well.

I believe the Scriptures are true. I trust my eternal salvation into the words of its pages: my life depends on them. After my study of the Passover and resurrection events, I am convinced that Jesus died on Thursday. I'm also convinced that history records Jesus as being born somewhere between 4BC and AD3. If history is remotely close, within 12 years, the only dates Jesus could have died are between AD26 and AD38. There is only one day in that entire period that could be a Thursday full moon, making the crescent visible two weeks prior on a Friday. I confirmed this possibility using multiple resources. Because I believe Scripture is true, I believe if it were possible to accurately calculate the new moon, we would find the crescent visible on March 24, AD30.

Having declared my outcome and reasoning, I only include the following observations and thoughts as a way to show you the types of efforts I engaged to help shape my understanding in an attempt to prove or disprove the Thursday Passover. On all fronts, I failed to disprove it. I cannot underscore enough that my final outcome is the paragraph above, because the more I dug into a mathematical or analytical way to *prove* the crescent moon date, I ran into item after item that could be an interfering event. With these comments out of the way, here are my findings in hopes that if you attempt to calculate a date, you will learn from what I did and either correct my mistakes or springboard off my findings.

My Attempt to Calculate All Crescent Dates on Fridays

The first day of any given month in Judaism was established by the first visible lunar crescent. It had to be viewed and testified by multiple people. When spotted, it was testified to the temple leaders and they would declare the beginning of the new month. A crescent on Friday would allow for a Thursday Passover sacrifice.

After much research, I wonder how possible it really is to calculate the Gregorian date of the Passover for the following reasons:

- The lunar process is not consistent to the degree necessary in order to calculate an accurate position of the moon or how long it took on that given year. While it is true that the average lunar month is 29.530587981 days (29 d 12 h 44 min 2.8016 s), the longest can be 29.530588853 days and the shortest can be 27.554549878 days and it is understood that the calculable lunar cycle slips by an average of 2 seconds per year.

- Depending on the perigee and apogee of any given lunar cycle, the following cycle is different. Because gravity is an understood constant force, we believe it possible to be nearly correct on our calculations, however, "nearly" is enough to be wrong and a miscalculation by as little as an hour over 2,000 years could affect the outcome.

- We have no way to account for variations in lunar orbit based on meteorite impact (possibly pushing the moon in a given direction and/or increasing or decreasing its velocity) or other anomalies such as asteroids passing by closely enough that the gravitational pull of the meteor could have adjusted the velocity or trajectory of the moon, albeit slightly. Even if these events are small, one happening the day the crescent should be visible could affect it, even though the average would compensate over millennia.

To begin, we have to agree on the assumption that the average lunar month is self-correcting and established by God, meaning consistent, and that the anomalies discussed above are infrequent enough that the average would win, and that nothing happened the day's precluding the new crescent. An email conversation with the astronomy department of Oklahoma State University revealed an understood 2 second discrepancy in lunar cycle calculations every year. Going back 2,000 years creates a possible margin of error of +- 3hours, which is enough to affect the visibility of a crescent moon. Further, the university confirmed that items such as ambient light, earth surface heat, and myriad other interactions can impede any individual from seeing a new crescent. Without knowing all the intervening factors, it seems impossible to really know when the crescent is visible.

From the vernal equinox, the new visible crescent may become visible as early as 15 hours later, depending on local geography, surface temperature of the earth and numerous interacting forces. In AD30, the vernal equinox is calculated to have happened at 8PM JST on Wednesday, March 22nd in Jerusalem. That makes the first crescent visible on March 24th and that the first day of the month as well.

Moon Phases

Consider the following lunar shots retrieved from NASA. These shots show us what the crescent would look like in a purely dark and cold environment with no visual items interfering and the horizon not part of the equation. At exactly one day after the new moon convergence, 1.7% is visible and it looks like this:

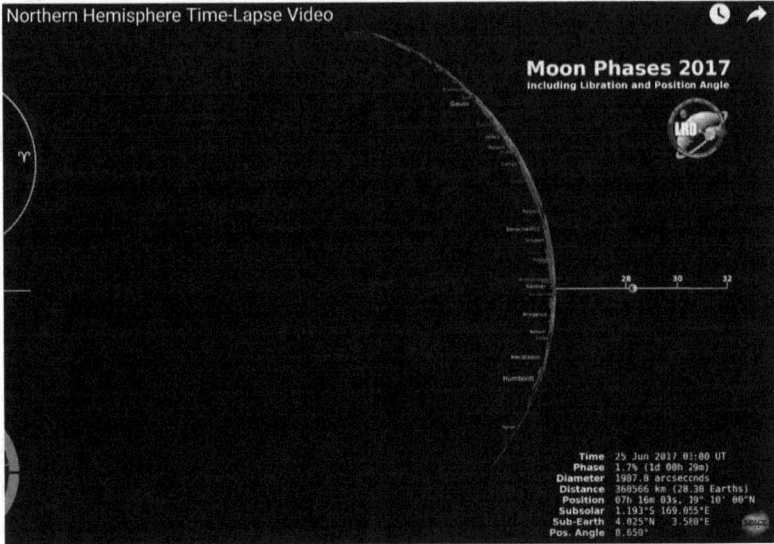

Image retrieved from VideoFromSpace https://www.youtube.com/watch?v=bZbPrm8_4bk

At 1 day and 7.5 hours after the full moon, 2.7% of the new moon is visible and this is the appearance:

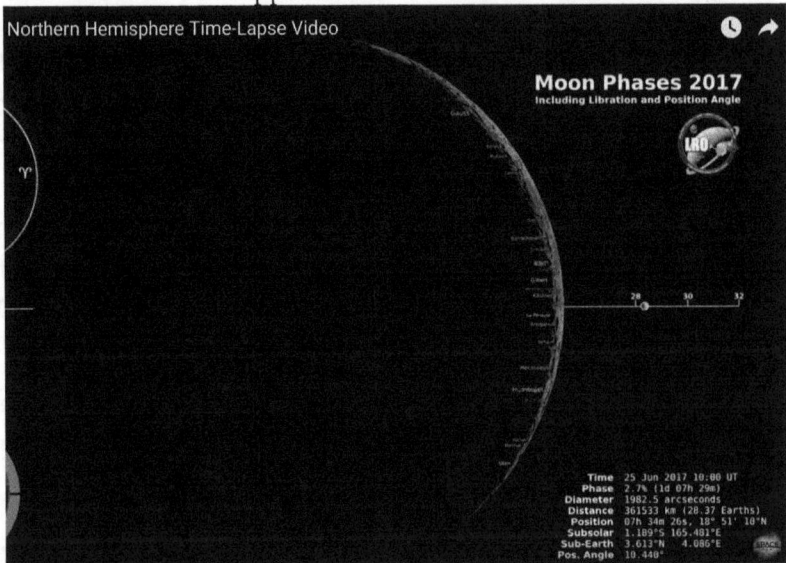

Image retrieved from VideoFromSpace https://www.youtube.com/watch?v=bZbPrm8_4bk

The new moon and the full moon are important pieces of the Passover calculation. The new moon of the vernal equinox in AD30 happened on March 22 at 6:20PM and April 6 at 8:16PM was the full moon.

We travel through the Jewish March 23rd Thursday evening and Jewish March 23rd Thursday morning (the evening and the morning are a day) and we arrive one day later at the beginning of a new day, which starts at Jewish Friday evening, March 24 at 5:52PM when the sun sets. Then, when we add 7.5 hours to that which brings us to 3:22AM and we are still in Friday evening to the Jewish calendar because the day doesn't advance until the sunset yet to come and we still haven't reached sunrise which begins the second half of Friday, so we must now traverse from 3:22AM until 5:22PM before the Jewish day of Friday is done. From the beginning the Jewish Friday evening, March 24 at 5:52PM and until the sunrise at 5:41AM (still Friday, March 24rd to the Jewish calendar), the moon would be visible for a number of hours, which would make the first day of the month March 24, 30AD which is a Friday and 13 days later would be the 14th of Nisan and that would be a Thursday.

Consider the following chart of data retrieved from the US Navy Military website that displays historical dates for new moons.

Year	New Moon	Convergence	Weekday
26	April 20	12PM	Sat.
27	April 9	4PM	Wed.
28	March 29	3AM	Mon.
29	April 17	3AM	Sun.
30	April 6	8PM	Thu.
31	March 27	11AM	Tue.
32	April 14	9AM	Mon.
33	April 3	3PM	Fri.
34	March 23	3PM	Tue.
35	April 11	8AM	Mon.
36	March 30	2PM	Fri
37	April 18	12PM	Thu.
38	April 8	3AM	Tue.

Data retrieved from https://aa.usno.navy.mil/

Because Passover is the 14th day of the first month, and the first month is based on the earliest visible crescent, that equates to Passover being on a full moon. When looking at the dates and times for the full moon and considering that the full moon must happen after 6PM on a Thursday (putting the initial crescent back exactly two weeks and visible on a Friday, there is no other date between AD26 and AD38. The only conflicting date AD 37, but it is too early in the day for the crescent to be seen 14 days prior.

Also, consider the following excerpts from various online resources:

> So what is the youngest moon you can see with your eye alone?
>
> How young a moon you can expect to see with your eye depends on the time of year and on sky conditions. It's possible to see the youngest moons – the thinnest crescents, nearest the sunset – around the spring equinox. That would be March for the Northern Hemisphere or September for the Southern Hemisphere...[and] Stephen James O'Meara [is recorded] in May 1990 [of seeing] the young crescent with the unaided eye 15 hours and 32 minutes after new moon.
>
> https://earthsky.org/astronomy-essentials/young-moon-visibility)

> The Jewish Encyclopedia states:
>
> The Sanhedrin was assembled in the courtyard ("bet ya'azek") of Jerusalem on the 30th of each month from morning to evening, waiting for the reports of those appointed to OBSERVE the new moon
>
> "New Moon," p. 243. See also Mishnah R.H.i.7, ii. 5-7; Sanh. 102.

As the Encyclopedia Judaica notes:

> Originally, the New Moon was not fixed by astronomical calculators, but was solemnly proclaimed after witnesses had testified to the REAPPEARANCE of the crescent of the moon. On the 30th of each month, the members of the high court (Sanhedrin) assembled in a courtyard in Jerusalem, named Beit Ya'azek, where they waited to receive the testimony of two reliable WITNESSES; they then sanctified the New Moon. If the Moon's crescent was not seen on the 30th day, the new moon was automatically celebrated on the 31st day"
> "New Moon," p. 1039.

If you are interested in astronomy, here are some additional items I uncovered during my research that you may find interesting.

Following are the perigees and apogees as calculated for AD30. The perigee is the closest part of the orbital ellipse of the moon's journey around the earth. The apogee is the furthest part of the moon's journey around the earth. There are speed differences on approach and departure toward and through both perigee and apogee. These must be considered when calculating a moon position and its visibility. This changes every month and is statistically improbable (if not impossible) to be the same between any two lunar cycles.

Perigees and Apogees

Perigee	Apogee
	Jan 1 14:12 404433 km F-7d 0h
Jan 15 9:26 370241 km F+6d18h	Jan 29 11:17 404402 km N+6d21h
Feb 10 7:30 366163 km F+3d 3h	Feb 26 6:06 405113 km N+5d 1h
Mar 10 5:51 360957 km F+1d15h	Mar 25 19:38 406015 km - N+2d23h
Apr 7 13:49 357687 km F+ 15h	Apr 22 1:05 406501 km -- N+ 12h
May 5 23:57 357164 km + F- 5h	May 19 4:46 406318 km - N-1d22h
Jun 3 8:28 359387 km F-1d 4h	Jun 15 15:48 405501 km N-4d 2h
Jul 1 10:54 363707 km F-2d 9h	Jul 13 7:59 404541 km N-5d23h
Jul 28 17:10 368580 km F-4d12h	Aug 10 2:42 404115 km N-7d16h
Aug 22 16:26 369094 km N+4d21h	Sep 6 22:26 404545 km F+6d 4h
Sep 18 17:30 364140 km N+2d11h	Oct 4 17:01 405495 km F+4d 7h
Oct 16 21:11 359292 km N+1d 4h	Nov 1 5:07 406221 km + F+2d 1h
Nov 14 8:44 356839 km -- N+ 5h	Nov 28 5:35 406349 km + F- 17h
Dec 12 22:01 357694 km N- 16h	Dec 25 11:21 405908 km F-3d 7h

Retrieved from https://www.fourmilab.ch/earthview/pacalc.html

Consider the following comparison between AD30 and 2012 where the new moon, full moon, equinox, apogees and perigees of the years are calculated to be very close (236km different on apogee and 1,442km different at perigee).

A review of the lunar cycles at the vernal equinox in 2012 shows that the speed to get from 1.7% at apogee (begins at 1d 8h 30m after new moon) to 2.7% at apogee (begins at 1d 18h 30m) is 10 hours as opposed to going from 1.7% at perigee (begins at 0d 23h 29m) to 2.7% at perigee (begins at 1d 7h 29m) making the elapsed time at perigee 8 hours. If the new moon was at 8PM Jewish Thursday, 1% of the moon is visibly by sunset Jewish Friday, but 3% of it would be visible by early morning. If we use the 2012 lunar cycle as the example, because it is so closely related to the AD30 lunar cycle, we can watch the crescent appearance unfold.

All the date/time combinations in green/gray below, appear as possible times that a new moon would be visible by the human eye in AD30 based on the similar data observations from NASA in 2012. All times were acquired by watching the NASA moon footage and recording the statistics.

Year	Apogee Date	Full/New	Apogee KM	NewMoon	Perigee	Full/New	Perigee KM	New Moon Date	Full Moon Date	Time between New and Full	Possible Comparison Years
2016	03/25/2016 14:17:00	F+	406123	+2d 2h	3/10/16 7:03	N+	359506	03/09/2016 01:56:00	03/23/2016 12:02:00		1897
2003	04/04/2003 04:32:00	N+	406209	+2d 9h	3/10/03 18:58	F+	359817	04/01/2003 19:21:00	04/16/2003 19:37:00		1870
0030	01/25/0030 19:38:00	N+	406015	+2d 23h	3/10/30 5:51	F+	360057	03/22/0030 20:20:00	04/06/0030 22:16:00	15d 1h 56m	1835+
2012	03/26/2012 06:05:00	N+	405779	+3d 15h	3/10/12 10:03	F+	362399	03/22/2012 14:39:00	04/06/2012 19:20:00	15d 4h 41m	1817+
1817	03/20/1817 16:59:00	N+	408112	+2h 19m	3/5/1817 3:00	F+	360570	03/17/1817 21:19:00	4/1/1817 23:13:00	15d 1h 54m	1582
2118	03/25/2118 10:15:00	N+	408018	+3h 4m	3/9/18 18:57	F+	361514	03/22/2118 08:06:00	04/06/2118 09:20:00	15d 3h 14m	2118
								0030	03/25/0030 19:38:00	01/00/1900 04:00:00		1490

Start Near New Moon*	KM	Crescent Visible	Dates in AD30**		
03/22/2012 15:00:00	400832	0.20%		3/24/30 sunset 5:53PM sunrise 5:38AM	
03/22/2012 19:00:00	401229	0.20%		3/24/2013 sunset 5.53 sunrise 5:37AM moonrise 6:15 moonset 7:42 at 5:53 its 21deg and 3.2% bright	
03/22/2012 23:00:00	401615	0.30%			
03/23/2012 03:00:00	401987	0.40%			
03/23/2012 06:59:59	402345	0.59%			
03/23/2012 07:00:00	402346	0.60%	03/22/2012 20:38:00 Jewish 23rd	Given that the difference between New Moon and Full Moon in AD30 is 15d 1h 56m	
03/23/2012 11:00:00	402691	0.80%	03/23/2012 00:38:00 Jewish 23rd	And given the difference between New Moon and Full Moon in 2012 is 15d 4h 41m	
03/23/2012 15:00:00	403021	1.10%	03/23/2012 04:38:00 Jewish 23rd	And given the difference in travel time between AD30 and 2012 is only 2h 45m	
03/23/2012 19:00:00	403337	1.40%	03/23/2012 08:38:00 Jewish 23rd	And given the new is earlier in 2012 by 5h 41m compared to AD30	
03/23/2012 23:00:00	403637	1.80%	03/23/2012 12:38:00 Jewish 23rd	And given the full moons earlier in 2012 by 2h 56m compared do AD30	
03/24/2012 03:00:00	403920	2.20%	03/23/2012 16:38:00 Jewish 23rd	And given that the maximum apogee is only 236km further out in AD30 than in 2012	
03/24/2012 07:00:00	404186	2.70%	03/23/2012 20:38:00 Jewish 24th	And given that reaching the maximum apogee is only 10h 27m longer in 2012 than in AD30 (making AD30 a faster maximum turnaround)	
03/24/2012 11:00:00	404435	3.30%	03/24/2012 00:38:00 Jewish 24th	And given that reaching the minimum perigee is only 7h 48m longer in 2012 than AD30 (making AD30 a faster approach to Apogee)	
03/24/2012 15:00:00	404665	3.80%	03/24/2012 04:38:00 Jewish 24th	And given that the minimum perigee is only 1,442km longer in 2012 than AD30	
03/24/2012 16:00:00	404720	4.00%	03/24/2012 05:38:00 Jewish 24th		
03/24/2012 19:00:00	404877	4.50%	03/24/2012 08:38:00 Jewish 24th	It seems believable that the Jewish 24th day would fall between 1.1% and 4.5% of the crescent moon	
03/24/2012 23:00:00	405068	5.10%	03/24/2012 12:38:00 Jewish 24th	which would be visible as a +-3% crescent in the morning or a +-4% crescent in the evening of the 24th	
03/25/2012 03:00:00	405239	5.80%	03/24/2012 16:38:00 Jewish 24th	when one compares the AD30 approach from perigee was faster due to the catapult of the earth's gravity	
03/25/2012 04:00:00	405278	6.00%	03/24/2012 17:38:00 Jewish 24th	and that the perigee was shorter for the turn around, the speed plus the shorter distance should	
03/25/2012 08:00:00	405425	6.80%	03/24/2012 21:38:00 Jewish 25th	account for a quicker turn at perigee	
03/25/2012 12:00:00	405545	7.60%	03/25/2012 01:38:00 Jewish 25th		
03/25/2012 16:00:00	405644	8.40%	03/25/2012 05:38:00 Jewish 25th	Even moving the AD30 dates up into the earlier 2012 new moon range to split the difference of the	
03/25/2012 20:00:00	405720	9.30%	03/25/2012 09:38:00 Jewish 25th	2012 longer cycle gives us between a 1.8 and a 2.2% crescent in the early morning and a 4-4.5% crescent before	
03/26/2012 00:00:00	405772	10.30%	03/25/2012 13:38:00 Jewish 25th	evening and the advent of the next day.	
03/26/2012 04:00:00	405799	11.20%	03/25/2012 17:38:00 Jewish 25th		
03/26/2012 08:00:00	405803	11.70%	03/25/2012 19:38:00 Jewish 26th		

And here, I stopped. It became very obvious that it would be near impossible to "prove" a crescent was visible or not because there were too many possible interfering factors; and short of a historical record identifying when it was visible, we were not there. Mathematically, it seems very believable and even more so by observing the moon cycle in 2012 that was so close to the AD30 cycle.

My final outcome, however, is not dependent on splitting seconds or really much of the investigation I shared above, but on a belief in the accuracy of Scripture. I believe the gospel accounts of the Passover and crucifixion show plainly that Jesus died on Thursday between 2:45PM and 3:50PM and that Passover lambs were sacrificed that same time period of the same Thursday. Given any calculation within a multiple hour discrepancy, there is only one year in the twelve possible years of Jesus adult life where the Passover can fall on a Thursday, and that is April 6, AD30. In absence of any valid competing Thursdays during the historical life of Jesus, it leaves only one conclusion: it must be *that* Thursday.

Chapter End Notes/Observations

ABOUT THE AUTHOR

Buck Hurlbut is an award-winning author as well as a systems and organizational analyst who has studied the Bible for more than 40 years. Through his analytical gifts and skills, he helps his readers understand people, organizations, processes and the events with which they interact. Buck invites interaction with his readers via his website at http://www.bucks.life.

Notes

---

i   For more on time, research the halachic hour.

ii   https://www.chabad.org/calendar/zmanim_cdo/locationid/247/locationtype/1

iii   For more on Jesus' head cloth, research the Sudarium of Oviedo

iv   For extra-biblical reading on Jewish burials in the first century, view Ada Grossi's work titled "Jewish Shrouds and Funerary Customs," a copy of which may be available at https://www.academia.edu/2427474

v   Read the introduction to "English Explanation of Mishnah Moed Katan" at https://www.sefaria.org/English_Explanation_of_Mishnahh_Moed_Katan.3.8.3?ven= Mishnahh_Yomit_by_Dr._Joshua_Kulp&lang=bi

vi   https://www.chabad.org/library/article_cdo/aid/526872/jewish/Hours.htm

vii   https://www.sefaria.org/Mishnah_Pesachim?lang=bi

viii   https://www.sefaria.org/Mishnah_Pesachim.4?lang=bi

ix   https://www.sefaria.org/Mishnah_Pesachim.5.4?lang=bi&with=all&lang2=en

x   https://www.sefaria.org/Mishnah_Pesachim.7.7?lang=bi&with=all&lang2=en

xi   https://www.sefaria.org/Mishnah_Pesachim.10.1?lang=bi&with=all&lang2=en

xii   https://www.sefaria.org/Mishnah_Pesachim.10.8?lang=bi&with=all&lang2=en

xiii   https://www.sefaria.org/Mishnah_Pesachim.5.1?lang=bi&with=all&lang2=en

xiv   For additional reading, the Passover sacrifice was traditionally expected after the evening sacrifices at the 8½ hour. Read Mishnah Pesachim 5:1,3 – https://www.sefaria.org/Mishnah_Pesachim.5?lang=bi

xv   https://www.sefaria.org/Mishnah_Pesachim.5.3?lang=bi&with=all&lang2=en

xvi   https://www.jewishvirtuallibrary.org/tamid

xvii   https://www.sefaria.org/Yevamot.66b.8?lang=bi&with=all&lang2=en

xviii   https://www.sefaria.org/Shulchan_Arukh%2C_Yoreh_De'ah.362.2n

xix   https://www.sefaria.org/English_Explanation_of_Mishnah_Moed_Katan.3.8.2

xx   Watch this video on the Shroud of Turin for more background: https://vimeo.com/159184788

xxi   See Appendix B for an informal learning attempt and conversation about this topic.

xxii   Likely due to the fast of the firstborn and the seudah hamafseket